An Illustrated Guide to

Angel Therapy

An Illustrated Guide to

Angel Therapy

Denise Whichello Brown

GRAMERCY BOOKS • NEW YORK

This 2001 edition is published by Gramercy Books™, an imprint of Random House Value Publishing, Inc., 280 Park Avenue, New York, NY 10017, by arrangement with D&S Books, Cottage Meadow, Bocombe, Parkham, Bideford, Devon, England, EX39 5PH.

Gramercy Books™ and design are trademarks of Random House Value Publishing, Inc.

Printed in Singapore.

Random House
New York • Toronto • London • Sydney • Auckland

A catalog record for this title is available from the Library of Congress

ISBN: 0-517-16397-7

987654321

Contents

Introduction

How I Came to Write This Book

I have so far written fourteen successful books on complementary therapies – primarily on massage, aromatherapy, and reflexology – but this is the book that I always knew was in my heart!

My first angelic encounter took place many years ago, during a particularly stressful time of my life. In desperation, I ran into a nearby church and asked for help, and the angels answered my prayers (as they always do). Since then, the angels have guided, inspired, and protected me in my life as a healer and teacher. This is the work that I was "born" to do, although it was not until my experience with the angels during my twenties that I at last discovered my soul's true pathway. As a young child, I distinctly remember looking at my hands inquisitively, "knowing" that they were meant for a "special" purpose. People used to admire them and remark that perhaps I should play the piano, but I knew that that was not what they were intended for! It was the angels who raised my spiritual consciousness, made me aware of my healing hands, and gave me a new sense of direction.

As for this book, the angels have been "nudging" me for some time now to write it. Since I did not respond to their requests, their presence has been increasingly in evidence in my treatment room. Many patients, including some extremely down-to-earth individuals, touched by their radiance, have suddenly, tentatively, asked me if I know anything about angels. Many have clearly sensed their presence or have even seen these angelic beings. So this book is finally here, thanks to a culmination of "human" and "angelic" intervention!

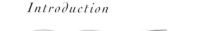

Connecting and Working With Angels

Nowadays, our fascination with angels is becoming more and more evident. Humanity is beginning to work in much closer cooperation with the angels. Angel books, tapes, and workshops are on the increase and angels now feature extensively in movies, on television, in newspapers and magazines, and in popular music. Large numbers of people claim to have experienced some kind of angelic encounter. In fact, I would go so far as to suggest that every one of us will have **at least** one angelic encounter at some point in our lives!

Do not imagine that it is necessary to be a clairvoyant or a medium to experience the joy of angels. The veil that separates us from the angelic kingdom is very thin. All that we need to do is to lift this veil in order to see their world revealed to us in all of its wondrous glory. You do not even actually have to "see" angels to experience them. The majority of us are aware that we are never completely alone and feel their beautiful presence enfolding and guiding us, bringing us comfort, wisdom, and healing.

I sense the presence of angels very strongly on a daily basis – very much so as I am writing this book! Whenever I request their help in my work as a practitioner of complementary medicine, they always come to assist me. Personally, I do not usually see

Beautiful angelic ornaments will inspire and delight.

them in an "angelic form," and I suspect that this is because angels only assume a particular form for our benefit and, as I already recognize their presence, they have no need constantly to manifest themselves to me. As I work, however, I often see their different-colored beams of light descending upon my patients. Patients have given me many descriptions of the angels who help their healing processes, and each patient's description is slightly different. However, all agree that when angels are present there is an incredible and overwhelming sense of peace and love. The beauty of the moment is simply breathtaking.

In this book, I hope to teach you how you, too, can bring the love and joy of angels into your daily life. You will discover ways of connecting and working with your angels. They can assist us in so many ways: they can help to heal us on physical, emotional, and spiritual levels, bring inspiration and guidance, solve problems, provide protection, improve relationships, and generally make life a whole lot easier. All we have to do is ask!

Representations of angels can be found in and on many everyday items.

What are Angels?

The word "angel" is derived from the Greek word *angelos*, meaning "messenger." Angels can be thought of as "divine messengers" or "messengers from God." Since they emanate from the divine source, it is through the angels that we have a special link with God. He created these wondrous beings to guide, protect, and inspire us. Their purpose is to serve us and to encourage us to grow and expand our consciousness.

Angels exist on a different vibrational frequency, which is why we are unable to perceive them ordinarily. The angelic rate of vibrational frequency is more etherealized than that of current humanity. As our own frequencies start to shift, we become able to perceive the etheric realms more easily and clearly. However, angels can appear to us in a myriad of ways that are personal to each individual. Many people "sense" their presence, some hear them, whilst others encounter them in dreams and visions. Angels are all around us, watching over us, and we can call upon them at any time. The hierarchy of angels is a practical reality at our disposal. These entities evolve by serving humanity, and by calling upon angels we are therefore helping them, as well as ourselves! Do not wait for a time of crisis or sorrow before invoking them. Invite them to become a part of your everyday life now. They are eagerly waiting to be called into service.

Angels are **not** part of the human stream of conciousness and have therefore never incarnated in human form and never will. Angels never become humans (although they may assume human form temporarily) and humans never evolve into angels. This is in contrast to what are known as our "guides," who, on the other hand, **have** been incarnate (i.e., have lived upon this planet as humans).

In fact, it is highly likely that you will have met one or more of your guides (we usually have several guides) in previous incarnations. A spirit guide may be a deceased loved one, such as a parent or grandparent, who passed away when you were young or even before you were born. You have different guides as you progress through your spiritual life. You can "feel" the difference between an angel and a guide: angels have a higher vibratory energy frequency.

Angels are genderless beings since they possess both male and female qualities. One person may perceive a particular angel or archangel as female, whereas another individual will see this same being as male. They are actually androgynous beings, with their masculine and feminine aspects in perfect balance.

We all have our own, special **guardian angel** who journeys with us throughout **all** of our numerous incarnations. This one loves us unconditionally and knows us inside out. We also have another accompanying personal angel, who works alongside our guardian angel, but is only present for **one** incarnation. This angel is present with you from the moment that the soul decides to reincarnate until the point of death. This angel will accompany you through this lifetime, through all of your trials and tribulations, but will not be present the next time you incarnate. In your next incarnation, a different angel will accompany you. An angel who is specific to a particular incarnation will be very attuned to that particular lifetime. For instance, in my case, my angel is highly experienced in the healing arts. I often find that I "know" a great deal about therapies that I have not studied in this lifetime.

Each of us has our own Guardian Angel who watches over us.

The Angelic Hierarchy

Elementals and devas are part of the angelic hierarchy.

The lowest manifestations are the **elementals**. These may appear to humans as simple specks or flashes of light or color or they may appear as fairies, elves, gnomes, sylphs (air spirits), salamanders (fire spirits), or undines (water spirits). These beings are closely connected with nature and the elements.

Devas are evolved elementals, and their purpose is to guard large forests, rivers, and so on, as well as to oversee the seasons. They are also very abundant at sacred sites and buildings, along with holy shrines.

It is from these devic beings that the angels evolve.

The Evolution of Angels

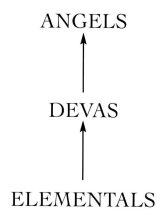

ANGELS

↑

DEVAS

↑

ELEMENTALS

According to several angel historians, there are three categories, or spheres, of angelic beings.

SPHERE 1

These angels serve as heavenly counsellors and are closest to God.
1. Seraphim
2. Cherubim
3. Thrones

SPHERE 2

These angels serve as heavenly governors.
1. Dominions
2. Virtues
3. Powers

SPHERE 3

These angels serve as heavenly messengers.
1. Principalities
2. Archangels
3. Angels (most connected to the physical world)

There are seven ranks of celestial beings mentioned in the New Testament – thrones, dominions, virtues, powers, principalities, archangels, and angels. In the Old Testament, cherubim and seraphim are found.

Sphere 1
Heavenly counsellors

Seraphim

The seraphim are considered the highest order of the angelic hierarchy. These highly evolved beings are the closest to God and are thought to surround the throne of God, working with sound and singing the music of the spheres. They constantly sing God's praise. They balance the movement of the planets, stars and the heavens by using sound.

In the Old Testament, the seraphim are described as flaming creatures because they are aflame with love. 'Round him flaming creatures were standing, each of which had six wings. Each creature covered its face with two wings and its body with two, and used the other two for flying.' (Isaiah 6.)

Seraphim are described as 'flaming creatures'.

As the guardians of light, Cherubim guard the light emanating from the sun, moon and stars.

Cherubim

The cherubim are the guardians of light, which emanates from the sun, the moon and the stars. They are the second-highest order of angels and their name stands for 'one who prays' or 'wisdom'. They are depicted on the Ark of the Covenant as its guardians and are also known as the record-keepers of heaven. They are not cute and cupid-like, as portrayed by a succession of painters.

Thrones

Thrones are the third-ranking order and are the angels of the planets. Each planet has its own throne – the guardian of our planet is the earth angel. They are known as the 'many-eyed ones' and 'wheels' and are believed to be charioteers around the Throne of God. In Ezekiel I, they are described as having 'four faces and four wings'.

Each Throne guards a different planet. The Earth Angel is guardian of our planet.

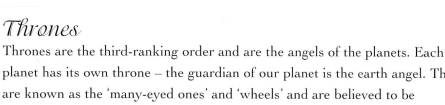

Sphere 2

Heavenly Governors

Dominions

The fourth-ranking order of angels, the dominions, are the governors or regulators of all of the angelic beings who are not as evolved as themselves. Their purpose is to advise the lower angelic groups. They have been depicted as carrying golden staffs in their right hand and the seal of God in their left.

Virtues

Virtues are the fifth-ranking order of angels. They are often referred to as the "brilliant" or "shining" ones since they are able to transmit enormous beams of divine light. They are thought to be the angels of miracles and blessings. The two angels present at the ascension of Jesus are believed to have been from the virtues.

Powers

Powers are the sixth-ranking order of angels. These may have been the first order of angels created by God. They protect our souls from evil beings and avenge evil in the world. The powers are believed to be the keepers of the Akashic records (i.e., the records of all of the thoughts and actions that occur during each soul's evolutionary journey). They oversee birth, death, and rebirth.

The Powers protect our souls and oversee birth.

Sphere 3

Principalities

The seventh-ranking order of angels, the principalities, are the overseers of large groups and organizations. They are believed to guard nations, cities, and also leaders. The angel who aided David when he slayed Goliath was thought to have come from this order.

Archangels

Archangels are the eighth-ranking order of angels and possibly the most widely known – Gabriel, Michael, and Raphael in particular. They will each be described in detail later on in this book.

Angels

The ninth-ranking order of angels, these are the closest to humanity. This group is made up of many different kinds of angel, with many different purposes. For instance, there are angels of joy, love, hope, healing, peace, and so on. Guardian angels are included in this category.

The principalities guard large organizations or groups. They oversee cities and nations.

Archangels

The archangels are also referred to as the "overlighting angels," since their function is to "overlight," or watch over and direct, groups of angels, as well as all aspects of humanity.

In the angelic hierarchy described previously, the archangels are the eighth-ranking order of angels and the most widely known. The three that you may be most familiar with, and who are mentioned in the Bible, are Michael, Gabriel, and Raphael.

These powerful beings of light respond to our calls the moment we ask for their assistance. Remember constantly to invite the archangels, as well as the angels, into your daily lives. God created them all to serve us. Each archangel has a particular function to fulfill, and it is useful to be aware of the main purposes of each archangel so that you know which one to call upon whenever you need assistance. Remember to summon the archangels to help others, as well as yourself.

Connecting With Archangels

At the end of each individual archangel section is a list of fiats. These are short, yet very powerful, affirmations, which can be repeated as often as necessary. Each time you say them you will be connecting more closely with the particular archangel.

Select the archangel whom you wish to invite into your life and choose the fiat that resonates most closely with you.

Spend a few minutes every morning and evening at your sacred altar repeating your chosen fiat. If you like, you can gradually increase the number of repetitions. Then just wait and see! Some people experience immediate results, whereas others have to be patient and wait for the desired changes to take place.

Using the Archangel Fiats

1. Sit in a comfortable position, with your back held straight.
2. Ground yourself by visualizing roots extending deep into the earth from the soles of your feet and the base of your spine.
3. Take a few deep breaths until you feel relaxed and calm.
4. Repeat your fiat.
5. Thank your chosen archangel.
6. Gradually open your eyes.

Of course, you may work with your archangels at any time you choose. If you wish, you can call on more than one at a time. In my work, I often use a combination of archangels. At the beginning of a treatment, I may ask for the protection of Archangel Michael to defend me from any unwanted negative energies. Then I may call upon Archangel Raphael and his team to assist me in my healing work. If I find that the person I am treating is depressed, I may call upon Chamuel. If their body is full of toxins, Archangel Gabriel can be summoned to help with the purification process. Finally, I may connect with Archangel Zadkiel and use his violet flame to transmute any negative energy into positive energy.

Other Archangels

The archangels whom I have described are known as the seven mighty archangels. However, there are many others whom you may encounter. For instance, Archangel Sandalphon who, it is said, Elijah became after his death. Archangel Sandalphon works with the earth energies and is particularly useful for grounding and anchoring energies into the earth. Sandalphon is the ultimate archangel for the earthly grounding of spiritual energies.

Metatron is yet another archangel who is believed to hold the highest rank. Metatron is a truly magnificent being, whom I am blessed to have channeled.

All angels and archangels are awaiting invocation. Let your intuition lead you toward the ones whom you need to guide you along your spiritual pathway. I strongly suggest that you make frequent use of these wondrous beings. Your life will never be the same again.

Michael is the most renowned of all of the archangels. Some consider Michael the leader of the archangels. He protects us physically, emotionally, and psychically.

Archangel Michael

Meaning of "Michael":

"Who is like God";

"Like unto God";

"Who is like the Divine."

Color:

blue/gold. Michael is often depicted with a sword, holding the scales of justice, or carrying the blue flame of protection.

Key words:

Michael is the archangel of:

protection;

courage/strength;

truth/integrity.

Protection

Archangel Michael protects us physically, emotionally, and psychically. Many people have experienced miracles after calling upon Michael and his angels of protection. Michael will protect you in many different situations.

- If your automobile has broken down late at night along a dark country lane.
- If you are alone in the house and are fearful of burglars.
- If you are embarking on a journey in your automobile.
- If you are in what you perceive to be an unsafe environment.
- If you are being physically attacked.
- If you are being sexually abused.
- If you are under psychic attack.
- If you have left a relationship and the other person will not "let go," you can ask Archangel Michael to cut through the etheric cords that bind you and the other person together.

Courage/strength

Archangel Michael gives us the courage to face any obstacle, no matter how insurmountable it may seem.

- If you are under severe mental strain – for instance, your job may be too demanding, involving deadlines that are impossible to meet – Michael will give you the courage to demand changes.
- If you are under emotional strain – for instance, in a relationship.
- If you feel that life is not worth living.
- If you have any addiction.
- If you are very ill and are suffering from a degenerative disease or even a terminal illness.
- If you suffer from nightmares.

Truth/integrity

Archangel Michael helps us to follow our truth without compromising our integrity. He helps us to find our true natures and to be faithful to who we really are. He can give assistance in many situations.

- If you are afraid to, or find it difficult to, tell the truth.
- If you are in a relationship that is not in your best interests and need to accept the truth.
- If you are only pretending to like your job.
- If you will not act on what you say.
- If you always say what others want you to.
- If you are in denial about anything and are unable to face the truth.
- If you have betrayed someone by not telling the truth.

Fiats to Archangel Michael

1. Archangel Michael. Help me! Help me! Help me!
2. Archangel Michael. Protect me from all harm!
3. Archangel Michael. Give me the courage to face this situation!
4. Archangel Michael. Help me to discover the truth!
5. Archangel Michael. Help me to be true to myself!

Raphael exudes the healing power of the divine.

Archangel Raphael

Meaning of "Raphael":

"Healing power of God";

"The Divine has healed";

"God heals".

Color:

green/deep pink. Raphael exudes the color of healing and of the heart chakra.

Key words:

Raphael is the archangel of:

healing;

wholeness/unity.

Healing

Raphael assists with all forms of healing – orthodox and complementary medicine alike. Archangel Raphael will help to heal body, mind, and spirit. Ask Raphael to intervene in the following instances.

- If you are sick or a loved one is ill.
- If you are undergoing surgery or treatment.
- If you are a therapist and need extra help or guidance.
- If you are searching for a therapist or even a school of complementary medicine.
- If you are a scientist searching for a medical cure.
- If you are a doctor or surgeon.
- If you are in pain, whether physical, emotional, or mental.

- If you need help to heal past wounds (physical, emotional, or mental).
- If a relationship needs repairing.

Wholeness/unity

Raphael can bring unity to your life. Call forth Raphael if the following happens to you.

- If you have had a shattering experience and need to be "pieced"/"peaced" back together again.
- If you feel out of touch with your spirituality.
- If your soul does not feel "whole."
- If you need unification of the physical, emotional, mental, and etheric bodies.
- If you have lost a partner and no longer feel "whole."
- If a relationship has broken down and you feel shattered. Please remember that when you make your requests to the archangels they are unable to interfere with your karma.

Fiats to Archangel Raphael

1. Archangel Raphael, heal my wounds of the past!
2. Archangel Raphael, help my body to heal!
3. Archangel Raphael, heal my wounded spirit!
4. Archangel Raphael, heal my physical/mental/emotional pain!
5. Archangel Raphael, help me to heal and restore my relationship with _____!
6. Archangel Raphael, make me whole again!
7. Archangel Raphael, assist me in my healing work!

Chamuel embodies the principle of pure,
unconditional love.

Archangel Chamuel

Meaning of "Chamuel":

"He who sees God."

Color:

pink/orange.

Key words:

Chamuel is the archangel of:
unconditional love;
relationships/making allowances/nurturing.

Unconditional love

The Archangel Chamuel embodies the principle of pure love and can lift you from the depths of sorrow. Call forth Chamuel in the following instances.

- If you find it difficult to love yourself.
- If you are unable to feel love for others.
- If your heart has hardened and is full of negative emotions, such as envy, guilt, bitterness, or lack of forgiveness.
- If your heart is blocked with depression, hopelessness, and despair.
- If you feel lonely and broken-hearted.
- If you are judgemental and cynical.

Relationships/making allowances/nurturing

Chamuel enables you to renew and improve existing relationships. Invoke Chamuel if the following apply.

- If you place conditions on your love: "I'll love you if you _____" or "I won't love you if you _____."
- If you have experienced the breakdown of a relationship.
- If you cling to your relationships and do not allow others the freedom to be able to express themselves freely.
- If you need to strengthen a parent-child bond.
- If you have lost someone close to you through death or separation.
- If you and your children have experienced a divorce.
- If you "need" to be loved.
- If you perform tasks for others conditionally in order to receive gratitude and acknowledgement.
- If you do not appreciate the love that you have in your life.

Fiats to Archangel Chamuel

1. Archangel Chamuel, fill my heart with your unconditional love!
2. Archangel Chamuel, guide me to feel love for others and myself!
3. Archangel Chamuel, remove the negativity from my heart!
4. Archangel Chamuel, heal the pain within my heart!
5. Archangel Chamuel, help me to strengthen my relationship with _____!
6. Archangel Chamuel, help me to let go of my relationship with _____!

Gabriel is well known as the archangel who told the Virgin Mary of the impending birth of the Son of God in the Bible. He revealed the purpose of her life to her and will help you to find your true calling.

Archangel Gabriel

Meaning of "Gabriel":

"Strength in God";

"The Divine is my strength";

"God is my strength."

Color:

indigo/white.

Key words:

Gabriel is the archangel of:

guidance;

vision/inspiration/prophecy;

purification.

Guidance

Archangel Gabriel helps us to find our true calling. Ask for Gabriel's guidance if the following applies to you.

- If you have strayed from your soul's pathway.
- If you wish to understand your life plan and purpose.
- If you can find no reason for being.
- If changes are ahead and you need guidance.
- If you are contemplating a house move or major purchase.
- If you are thinking of changing career.
- If you are establishing a new relationship.
- If you are considering starting a family.

Vision/inspiration/prophecy

Archangel Gabriel can bring messages to you just as he did to the Virgin Mary. Gabriel is also credited with inspiring Joan of Arc in her mission. Contact Gabriel:

- If your "third eye" is closed and your spiritual vision is therefore blocked.
- If you wish to receive visions of angelic guidance regarding the direction you are going in.
- If you wish to receive prophecies of the changes ahead.
- If you need help in interpreting your dreams and visions.

Purification

Archangel Gabriel can be called forth to awaken the purification process. This may need to be done to make way for changes. Call Gabriel forth:

- If your body is full of toxins and needs purifying.
- If your thoughts are impure or negative and need clearing and cleansing.
- If you have been raped or sexually assaulted and feel dirty.
- If you are, or have been, under psychic attack.
- If your house has been robbed and feels unclean.
- If your work/home/environment feels negative.
- If you feel that you have absorbed someone else's problems.

Fiats to Archangel Gabriel

1. Archangel Gabriel, guide me along my soul's pathway!
2. Archangel Gabriel, reveal to me my life's calling!
3. Archangel Gabriel, help me to interpret my visions!
4. Archangel Gabriel, inspire and guide me through the changes that lie ahead!
5. Archangel Gabriel, purify my body, mind, and spirit!
6. Archangel Gabriel, cleanse my body of toxic substances!
7. Archangel Gabriel, cleanse my mind of impure thoughts!
8. Archangel Gabriel, free me from psychic attack!

Jophiel will awaken a sleeping soul
from its slumber.

Archangel Jophiel

Meaning of "Jophiel":

"Beauty of God."

Color:

yellow.

Key words:

Jophiel is the archangel of:
awakening/wisdom;
illumination/inspiration;
joy.

Awakening/wisdom

Call on Archangel Jophiel:

- If your soul is sleeping and needs awakening so that you may take your first steps along your spiritual pathway.
- If you wish to awaken a deeper understanding of yourself.
- If you are seeking a connection with the higher self.
- If you are "blind" to the etheric realms.

Illumination/inspiration

Call forth Jophiel:

- If you wish to experience flashes of insight in which everything suddenly becomes clear.
- If you are searching for answers to the questions in your life.
- If you wish the greater wisdom to be revealed to you.
- If you have difficulty in understanding yourself and others.
- If you wish to throw some light on a difficult situation.
- If you need mental clarity (for example, when studying for an exam).

Joy

Call on Jophiel:

- If you feel that you have lost your inner light.
- If you need joy and laughter in your life.
- If the sunshine has gone out of your life (call on Jophiel if you suffer from seasonal affective disorder, S.A.D.).

Fiats to Archangel Jophiel

1. Archangel Jophiel, fill my body, mind, and spirit with light!
2. Archangel Jophiel, help me in my quest for enlightenment!
3. Archangel Jophiel, unveil the etheric realms!
4. Archangel Jophiel, reveal the greater wisdom to me!
5. Archangel Jophiel, fill me with joy and laughter!

Uriel will enable you to find
inner peace within yourself that
passeth all understanding.

Archangel Uriel

Meaning of "Uriel":

"The light of God";

"The light and fire of the Divine."

Color:

gold/purple.

Key words:

Uriel is the archangel of:

peace/tranquility;

giving/receiving/service/devotion.

Peace/tranquility

Archangel Uriel is associated with the solar plexus, where we store so much tension. Call Uriel forth:

- If you are unable to find inner peace.
- If you wish to let go of your inner turmoils and release your fears.
- If you wander from place to place, job to job, or relationship to relationship.

- If your relationships are volatile and full of disagreements.
- If you are full of anger and irritation.
- If you wish to bring peace to the world and to end wars and conflicts.

Giving/receiving/service/devotion

Call forth Uriel:

- If you are unable to give freely.
- If you give too much to the point of exhaustion.
- If you do things only for personal gain.
- If you have difficulty in receiving.
- If you wish to experience the pleasure of serving humanity.

Fiats to Archangel Uriel

1. Archangel Uriel, fill me with thy peace!
2. Archangel Uriel, release my fears!
3. Archangel Uriel, bring peace to the world!
4. Archangel Uriel, help me to serve others to fulfill thy divine purpose!

Zadkiel transforms us with the healing power of forgiveness and transmutes dense, negative energy into positive energy.

Archangel Zadkiel

Meaning of "Zadkiel":

"Righteousness of God."

Color:

violet.

Key words:

Zadkiel is the archangel of:
forgiveness/mercy/tolerance;
the transmutation of negative energy.

Forgiveness/mercy/tolerance

Forgiveness is a great healer – without it, negative energies, such as anger, hatred, and guilt, will build up and cause health problems. Invoke Archangel Zadkiel:

- If you are unable to forgive others.
- If you are unable to forgive yourself.
- If you feel anger, hate, bitterness, and resentment toward others.
- If you find it difficult to tolerate others.
- If you are unable to tolerate aspects of yourself.
- If you find it difficult to be tactful.

The Transmutation of Negative Energy

Archangel Zadkiel works with the high-frequency spiritual energy known as the "violet flame." This flame was brought down for us by Saint Germain. Saint Germain is an Ascended Master and Chohan (Lord) of the seventh great ray of energy emanating from the Creator. Connect with Archangel Zadkiel and Saint Germain:

- If you wish to transmute dense, negative energy into positive energy.
- If you wish to purify your body, mind, and soul.
- If you desire to remove the obstacles between yourself and God and to accelerate your spiritual development.
- If you wish to transmute your negative karma.
- If you want to heal any records of previous lives.
- If you wish to dissolve planetary karma that arises from wars and other negative events.

Fiats to Archangel Zadkiel

1. Archangel Zadkiel, help me to forgive _____!
2. Archangel Zadkiel, help me to forgive myself!
3. Archangel Zadkiel, assist me to develop tolerance toward myself and others!
4. Archangel Zadkiel, cleanse me with thy violet flame!
5. Archangel Zadkiel, transmute my negative karma!
6. Archangel Zadkiel, connect with me to dissolve our planetary karma.

Invoking and Communing With the Angelic Realms

Creating a Heavenly Environment

If you wish to establish a strong connection with the angelic realms, it is important to create a sacred space where you can commune with them. The more you raise the energetic vibrations in the space that you intend to use, the better the angels will like it!

Angels are attracted to places of peace, harmony, and love, and you should aim to create a peaceful and spiritual haven where you can completely relax, clear your thoughts, focus your mind, and open your heart to the angelic realms.

Purify the Environment

1. Clear Away the Clutter

This will help to dispel any negativity that may have accumulated. Angels are not drawn toward rooms full of junk. It will also clear your mind, as well as your home. You will feel much clearer and more energetic once you have got rid of the unwanted possessions around you. Discard any items that you have not used or worn in the past two years.

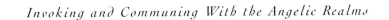

2. Clean the Room Thoroughly

As you do this, open the windows to allow the light to come streaming in. Play some uplifting music or, even better, chant the name of God. This will cleanse the room and help to purify, cleanse, and heal your physical, emotional, mental, and spiritual bodies. Everyone will have one or several particular names of God to which they will respond on a deep level. Let your intuition guide you. As you chant, experiment with different speeds, pitches, and volumes. You can chant slowly or quickly, high or low, loudly or softly – do whatever feels best for you. The most important thing is that you should chant with love in your heart. It is the vibration of love that will call the angels to you. Chants do not have to be incredibly complicated to be powerful. You may like to chant *Om Shanti*, which is a peace mantra, or *Hari Om*, which is a more energizing chant. Or you could simply repeat a word, such as "peace" or "love," over and over again. You could even chant one of the names of the archangels, such as Michael, Chamuel, Gabriel, or Raphael.

3. Smudge the Room

To cleanse a room thoroughly, smudge sticks are an excellent idea. In Native American spiritual traditions, smudging plays an important role. Smudge sticks are bundles of tightly bound plant material (sage is extremely purifying). To use a smudge stick, light it at one end, then blow out the flame so that the stick is just smoldering. Walk slowly around the room with your smudge stick, intuitively carrying it to any areas where you feel it is required, paying particular attention to the corners. If you wish, you can direct the smoke with your hand or a feather. It will only take a minute or two to smudge a room and afterwards the room will feel not only cleansed, but also much warmer.

4. Holy Water

You may also sprinkle holy or sacred water around your room to purify and lift the vibrations. I have recently mixed a wonderful combination of holy waters gathered from the well of Mother Meera in Germany, from the chalice well in Glastonbury, England, and from Lourdes in France. A very healing trinity of water! Only a few drops need to be sprinkled to change the vibrations dramatically.

Create an Angelic Altar

*O*nce the area has been cleansed, you can create your own altar in honor of your angels. Find a small table or box and cover it with a beautiful piece of fabric in your favorite color. Then place some of your most precious things on the altar: perhaps a statue or picture of your favorite angel or spiritual master, a crystal, a stone that you may have collected from a sacred place, some fresh flowers, a candle, a silk scarf, and a few essential oils. Frankincense, sandalwood, cedarwood, rosewood, myrtle, rose, and jasmine are all excellent essential oils to use in your spiritual practices. (These. and other oils. are detailed later in the book.) It is entirely up to you how you design your altar. Angels will be drawn to its beauty and love.

Try to spend a few minutes every day at your heavenly altar. Five minutes in the morning is a wonderful, positive way in which to start the day. Each time that you come to your altar you are consecrating your sacred space. It will store the energy that you create and this will make it easier for you to tune into the "angelic wavelength."

Purify Yourself

Self-purification will make it easier for the angels to communicate with you.

1. Purify Your Thoughts

It is no good appearing to be full of happiness and love on the outside whilst burying negative thoughts, such as jealousy, resentment, hatred, and fear, on the inside. You may be able to fool humans, but you will not deceive the angels! Your aura will be dark and dense if it is filled with negative thoughts. Try to fill your aura with thoughts of love, beauty, peace, and joy.

If you feel angry, frustrated, afraid, or worried, or have any negative emotions that you are having difficulty letting go of, write down these feelings on a piece of paper and then burn it. Fire is an incredibly powerful cleanser! I remember, many years ago, taking part in such a ceremony whilst on a Native American course in Spain. I burned all of the aspects that I wished to rid myself of and felt as if purification had taken place on a very deep level. It certainly had! On my return to England, a letter was awaiting me from a psychic in the United States who had carried out a reading for me six months prior to my vacation. She said that she had felt that she must write to tell me that something very powerful had occurred to me – the date that she referred to was the very day of the purification ceremony!

If it is not convenient to burn your piece of paper, then cut or tear it into pieces and bury it. I believe, however, that fire is the most effective method.

2. Smudge Your Aura

If you still intuitively feel that
there is negativity around
you, try using a sage smudge
stick to cleanse your aura.

3. Purify Your Body

Your body is the temple of your
soul and it does not appreciate, or
thrive upon, a diet of junk food. Your
taste buds may crave it, but poor-quality
food will lower your vibrations dramatically.
You do not have to be perfect, but try to
eliminate too much sugar, additives, salt,
alcohol, tea, coffee, red meat,
and dairy foods from
your diet. It is a
natural process
that, as your
body begins to
attune to the
higher
vibrational
frequency of the angels,
your desire and cravings for
inappropriate foods will lessen. You will want to
eat more natural foods and organic produce and will
naturally crave large quantities of pure, natural, spring water.

4. *Avoid Certain Places and People*

As you attune to the angelic realms, you may find that some of your friends and acquaintances will not appeal to you quite so much. If someone makes you feel drained or depressed, try spending less and less time with him or her for a while. What is happening is that you are absorbing their negative energies and are feeling bad. They, on the other hand, are absorbing your positive energies and are feeling wonderful!

You may also find that certain environments (such as smoky bars and noisy clubs) begin to lose their appeal. As I have said, however, you will find that this is a natural shift.

5. *Ask Your Angels*

If you still feel in need of cleansing, then, either in meditation or just before you go to sleep at night, ask the "angels of purification" to purify you as you sleep or mediate. Do this as often as is necessary and you will emerge feeling wonderfully clean and refreshed.

6. Call Upon Archangel Michael

If you feel that there is a person who is still holding on to you, perhaps from a past relationship, then call on Archangel Michael. Before you go to sleep, or in meditation, ask him to use his holy sword to cut the etheric cords that bind you and that are draining your energy.

Sensing the Presence of Angels

The angelic realms have many ways of making their presence known to us. As I have mentioned previously, angels exist on a different vibrational frequency to humans, and most of us are therefore unable to "see" them, although we can all at least "feel" their presence. It is not necessary to be deeply religious or to have a strong spiritual belief to sense the presence of an angel.

Below are a few "signs" that may indicate the presence of angels.

You may feel a change in temperature when an angel is present.

1. The temperature in the room may change. You may feel a rush of warm air or a warm glow surrounding you. You may also get goose bumps or a tingling at the back of your neck or head.

2. A mystical fragrance may appear from nowhere. It may be an aroma that you have never smelled before, and you will probably not be able to identify or describe the fragrance. The angels who work with me in my treatments carry with them the most exquisite aromas.

3. Different-colored lights may appear from nowhere. You may see shafts of light streaming down or shooting across the room or may catch glimpses of sparks of light or notice shadows. Do not be afraid: you will not see an angel appearing until you are ready to, and angels have no desire to alarm you.

4. You may "hear" angelic voices trying to "communicate" with you. This is called "clairaudience." If the voice is merely a whisper or is muffled, then ask your angel to speak louder. Do not assume that the angelic voice that you are hearing is mere fantasy or that you are on the road to insanity!

5. If you are clairsentient, you may experience sensations in your body, particularly in your heart. It is very common to be filled with an overwhelming sense of love and compassion when angels are around. Your eyes may fill with tears of joy and you may be unable to explain why.

6. White feathers may suddenly appear in the most unlikely and unexpected places. This is a sign that the angels are with you and are ready to answer your prayers.

7. Angels may appear to you in your dream state with a solution to a particular problem. By the morning, you will feel much more positive and clearer about which direction to take.

8. You may "feel" as though there is a presence in the room with you. You may feel as though "someone" has just brushed past you or may experience the sensation that a "presence" is standing behind you, perhaps with their hands on your shoulders.

9. Sometimes the angels will make their presence very obvious. A common experience often happens when you are in a bookstore: you are looking for guidance and a book will fall off the shelf as you walk by. This is the angels at work – trust in them and you will receive more and more signs.

All of these signs are very positive and desirable. They indicate that the angels are ready and waiting to serve you.

Invoking the Angels

The angels are awaiting your call, but they will not usually intervene in your life unless you request their assistance. They respect our free will and only on very rare occasions, in extreme emergencies, will they appear without being asked.

They are waiting to do your biding. However, any requests that you make must fulfill certain conditions.

1. Your requests must be positive.

2. They must not be harmful or hurtful to others.

3. They must not interfere with your karma. There are certain lessons that the soul needs to learn if progress is to be made in this lifetime. Our good and bad actions from this lifetime, and previous ones, will affect how the angels are able to respond to our prayers. However, they may be able to reduce the effects of our karma.

There are many ways to invoke your angels. Remember to go to the special, sacred place that you have created when you wish to communicate with them. Here are a few suggestions for how to work with the heavenly hosts.

1. Write to Your Angels

Sit down quietly in your spiritual haven, free from all distractions. Take the telephone off the hook and, if possible, lock the door to prevent interruption. Play some inspiring music, light a candle, and burn some essential oils.

Now pour out your heart to the angelic hosts. Even if you are feeling very agitated and irritated, it is amazing how quickly you calm down once you put pen to paper. Write down all of your problems and worries. Imagine that you are writing to your best friend. You will soon find that you are able to put everything into perspective.

Once you have written down your anxieties, you will feel much more positive and relaxed. Now hand over your burdens to your angels and ask them to find suitable solutions.
Finally, send those who have hurt and aggravated you thoughts of peace and love. You will be amazed by the results.

2. Mentally Call Your Angels

It is not always convenient to speak aloud to your angels: if you are at a business meeting, waiting for a bus, or in the supermarket, it could be very awkward! However, wherever you are, you can mentally ask your angels for assistance. Just think to yourself, "Angels, please help me." It is so simple and very effective.

3. Pray Aloud to Your Angels

You will receive a very powerful response if you speak aloud to your angels on a regular basis. We frequently call to the divine unconsciously, and if something goes wrong in our lives and we feel under stress, we regularly say "Oh my God" or "Jesus Christ!"

The more often you speak to your angels, the more effective your prayers will become. Each time you commune with the angels, the relationship that you have established grows stronger.

The power of your voice will amplify your requests. Even if you do not speak, the angels will still come, but it seems to be more effective if you speak aloud. Ask your angels for whatever help you need. You may ask the angels to protect your loved ones, and parents may ask for angels to protect their children (I do this every day when my children get on the school bus!) If you have friends who are struggling with problems, then ask the angels to comfort and advise them. Your friends do not have to believe in angels and also do not have to be aware that you are praying for assistance.

You can even pray for people whom you do not know. For instance, if you read about crimes or disasters, such as floods and earthquakes, invoke the light of the angels to heal and comfort those in distress.

4. Visualize Your Angels

You may visualize your angels in whatever physical form you desire – they are able to take on any form. Perhaps you see your angel as a brilliant ray of light or as a being with beautiful wings that enfold and protect you. We all have our own ideas.

This is how one of my patients describes her angel, the Archangel Michael: -

Very tall – 9 to 10 feet (2.7 to 3 meters).

Powerful, immensely strong.

He holds the massive sword of truth with both hands.

The sword point touches the ground. I am reminded of the cross – that which goes beyond earthly death and into the eternal light beyond.

The sword radiates sparks of light, all the colors of the rainbow – like shards of crystal.

He is surrounded by golden light that spreads outward and upward into infinity.

Dazzling white raiment (clothes/garment) – yet it does not hurt the eyes.

Soothing, gentle, peace.

Strong, powerful, caring, supporting, protection from all that is negative.

The voice is deep, resonating, and so confident, assertive, assuring.

Chloe-Jasmine Whichello (aged eleven) gives this description of her angel.

My Angel

Ariel soars high above the heavens, her golden wings flapping gently against the heavenly winds. Her golden hair cascades to her waist and her blue-green eyes sparkle as she brings more joy and love toward the world. Clothed in robes of purple satin, she protects the earth and all its inhabitants. The grass grows greener whenever she is near. The dark sky lightens as the sun blazes down on the world. May the rough sea be still and calm whenever she glides above it.

Ariel is my angel and she tries to protect me every day. She is in everyone, though everyone has their own special angel. Angels purify your spirit and encourage you to show the world what an amazing person you are. When Ariel sings, the moment the notes float out of her mouth heaven and earth tremble with the glorious singing. There is a place for everyone in heaven even if your spirit is bad. Angels accept anyone and that anyone is you. May you find your angel on your journey of enlightenment.

5. Dream With Your Angels

It is very effective to commune with your angels during your sleep. While we dream, there is a great deal of scope for interaction with the angelic kingdom. Why not invite the angels into your dreams nightly? It is so simple: as you lay your head on the pillow, either mentally or verbally say a prayer, such as the following: "Angels, please work with me in my dream state tonight. Help me to find which direction I should take."

You can, of course, be as specific as you want. If you are having problems with a relationship, for example, then call upon Archangel Chamuel and the angels of love for guidance.

6. Angel Cards

Angel cards are an excellent way of communing with the angelic realms and are also a lot of fun. You can purchase them in many bookstores, but it is often more effective to make your own. The very fact that you are creating a deck of cards for yourself will put you in touch with the angels. You are creating the opportunity for the angels to reach out to you and give you guidance. They provide a wonderful link with the angelic messengers and are an invaluable way of enhancing your intuition. They also allow you to focus upon particular aspects of your life and gain a deeper understanding of your inner self.

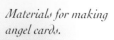

Materials for making angel cards.

You do not need to be an artist to make your own set of angel cards. To create your own cards, all that you need are several pieces of colored card and some pens or pencils. If you wish, use colored sequins or stars to enhance your cards. You can even buy images of small, shiny angels, snowflakes, and so on to stick onto your angel cards. On each of your cards, write the name of an angelic quality. There is no definite list of angelic qualities and I urge you to be creative. You may wish to include some of the forty qualities given in my list opposite. There is no minimum or maximum number of cards that you need to create for your deck: it is entirely up to you. Once you have made your angel cards, you may like to keep them in a special pouch, bag, box, or even just an envelope.

Angelic Qualities

Abundance
Adventure
Balance
Blessings
Communication
Courage
Creativity
Efficiency
Enthusiasm
Faith
Flexibility
Forgiveness
Freedom
Friendship
Harmony
Healing
Humor
Inspiration
Intuition
Joy

Light
Love
Patience
Peace
Play
Power
Purification
Purpose
Reliability
Responsibility
Romance
Simplicity
Spontaneity
Spiritual growth
Strength
Study
Synchronicity
Trust
Truth
Understanding

Ways of Working With Your Angel Cards

Before you begin, it is important to relax and center yourself. Breathe in peace and love and feel the tension dissolving from your body. Try using your cards in one of the following ways.

1. ATTUNING TO AN ANGEL

Place the deck of cards face down in front of you. Close your eyes and invite an angel into your life. Intuitively select a single card to which you feel drawn.

Take a few minutes to attune to the angel card that you have selected. Think about how it reflects upon your life.

Put your angel card somewhere where it is clearly visible, or carry it around with you, to remind you of the specific angelic quality that you have chosen.

2. ASKING A QUESTION

Shuffle the card deck thoroughly and, as you do so, ask the angels for help with a specific question. If you are clairsentient, you will "feel" when it is time to stop shuffling. If you are clairaudient, you will "hear" angelic voices telling you when to stop shuffling. If you are claircognisant, you will "know" when to stop. A clairvoyant will have a visual indication: for instance, one card may appear to be at a different angle from the others. Select one card to determine the response to your question.

3. "Past – Present – Future" layout

Shuffle the cards and, when you feel guided, lay them face down. Select three cards at random.

The card on the left reflects what has happened in the recent past, the middle card relates to the present, and the card on the right-hand side shows what the outcome may be. For instance, if you choose Friendship—Forgiveness—Harmony, this might suggest that a friend has let you down badly. The angels are here to teach you that you need to learn the lesson of forgiveness. If you can forgive them, your friendship will be harmonious once again. If you find it difficult to imagine, Archangel Zadkiel will assist you. With practice, you will find it easier to interpret the cards.

4. "What Should I Focus on?" Layout

Shuffle the cards and, as you do so, ask the angels what you should do next. Choose three cards and place them face up. The first card represents what you should focus on next. The second card reflects what the angels are trying to teach you. The third card is an indication of the outcome of the present situation. Suppose you chose Purification—Release—Spiritual growth, then the angels are asking you to focus on the purification of your life. This may involve giving up many bad habits and breaking away from old relationships. This will ultimately lead to a surge in spiritual growth.

5. "Physical – Emotional – Spiritual" Layout

Select three cards. The first card that you choose represents your physical alignment, the second card reflects your emotional state, and the third reveals your spiritual alignment.

6. FAMILY/GROUP GATHERINGS

At meal times with your family or friends, place a large basket on the table containing your cards. Let each person intuitively select which angel they will be drawing toward them for that day or the week to come.

7. ANGEL "CALENDAR"

On your birthday, or on New Year, choose twelve cards – one angel for each month of the year. Make a note of the angels that you have selected and notice how each one guides you through the coming months.

8. CHOOSE AN ANGEL PRIOR TO GOING TO SLEEP AND PLACE IT UNDER YOUR PILLOW TO INSPIRE YOUR DREAMS

We can gain a great deal of guidance and insight from our dreams. Keep a notebook beside your bed to record any parts of your dreams that you may feel are significant. Do not struggle to try to interpret your dreams – eventually the messages will become clear. Be patient!

9. INTUITIVELY SELECT AN ANGEL CARD FOR A FRIEND

It is not necessary for your friend to be present while you do this. Ask the deck for an angel who is available to assist your friend along the spiritual pathway or to help him or her with a specific problem.

Communing With Your Guardian Angel

For He shall give His angels charge over thee to guard you in all your ways.

PSALM 91:11.

Your guardian angel will accompany you throughout all of your incarnations, will guide you through all of your trials and tribulations, and will love you unconditionally, whatever you do.

We are usually only aware of our guardian angel in times of crisis, when, in desperation, we make an urgent plea for help. Remember: your guardian angel is **always** with you and is your bridge to the spiritual realm. The following exercise will enable you to connect with and draw your guardian angel closer to you. It is surprisingly easy to establish a connection with your angel. You do not have to be an expert in meditation: all that you need is the desire to attune to your angel. It is a wondrous and joyous experience to meet your guardian angel. Your relationship with your guardian angel will change your life and take you on a journey of spiritual discovery!

Preparation

Choose a time when you know that you will not be interrupted. Go to the special, sacred place that you have created – your angelic altar. Light a candle, incense stick, or essential-oil burner. Allow the wonderful aromas to diffuse into the atmosphere. Ensure that you are wearing comfortable and loose-fitting clothes. A loose T-shirt is ideal, but any clothes that are not constricting are suitable. For your comfort, have plenty of pillows around to allow you to feel relaxed during the angelic exercise. Have a blanket ready to wrap around you in case you start to feel chilly.

Keep an angel notebook and pen nearby to record any communication that you may receive. Use a "special" favorite pen (I have a wonderful one with pink hearts on it!) or maybe even keep a number of pens, each filled with a different-colored ink – each color for a particular angel. As you receive a message, make a note of the date. This will make it easier to refer to each transmission. When you come to reread them, you will realize just how accurate the messages are and will become aware of the huge benefit that you have derived from them. If you write down angelic messages, you are indicating to the angels that you appreciate and accept the information that you have been given. The more you acknowledge the messages, the more communications you will receive.

If you wish, you may play some beautiful music, or else you may prefer to sit in silence – personally, I find it easier to "hear" the angels in silence. Experiment and discover what works best for you.

Opening up to the Angelic World

You may wish to prerecord these instructions on tape when you first start this exercise. As you practice and familiarize yourself with it, you will find that you no longer need the tape.

1. Sit in a comfortable position. I find the ideal position is cross-legged on some pillows on the floor. However, if you prefer, you may perform this exercise sitting on a chair or a stool. It is important to hold your back straight so that you can ground yourself and establish a strong connection with the earth. This will make you feel safe, secure, balanced, focused, and receptive.

2. Focus your attention on your body and visualize roots coming out of the base of your spine (or from the soles of your feet if you are sitting on a chair or stool). Feel these roots growing and extending deep into the center of the earth, establishing a secure connection.

3. Become aware of your breathing and take a few deep breaths through your nose. Slowly inhale for a count of four and then hold the breath for a count of two. Exhale for a count of four and then pause for a count of two. Repeat this pattern (four – two – four – two) until you start to feel your mind emptying itself of all of its restless chatter. Allow any thoughts that pop into your mind to be released. Free your mind of its mental baggage.

4. As you inhale, feel your body overflowing with the beautiful, healing light of the angels. As you exhale, feel all of the tension dissolving from your body. Release any tension from your head, neck, shoulders, and back. Scan your body from the top of your head to the tips of your toes for any remaining tension. If you discover an area of tension, tighten the muscles of that area farther and then relax them as you exhale. With the out breath, you may like to give a deep sigh to rid yourself of any residual stress or toxins in your body. Allow it to be released through your "roots," all the way down into the center of the earth. As you breathe in healing light and exhale all of the tension from your body and mind, notice how relaxed and calm you feel.

5. When you are ready, bring your consciousness into your heart – this is where the angels connect with you. Place your hands on your heart area if you wish, and visualize a light deep within your heart. This is your divine spark. Connect with it.

6. When you feel deeply relaxed, say to yourself, "I am going to count to ten, and when I reach the number ten I will be in a state of heightened awareness in which I can communicate with the angelic realm." "One – two – three – four – five – six – seven – eight – nine – ten." Notice how connected you feel with the energies of heaven and your Creator, while at the same time remaining grounded in the earth energies.

7. Invite your guardian angel to draw closer to you. Imagine your angel beside you. If you are clairsentient, you may "feel" the gentleness and safety of its wings as it enfolds you. Perhaps you will become aware of an indescribable love in your heart. Experience the warmth in your heart as your heart opens, fills with unconditional love, and overflows with tenderness and compassion. "Feel" yourself being bathed and cherished by your guardian angel. If you are clairvoyant, you may "see" the most magnificent colors. Perhaps they are colors that you have never seen before. You may see your angel in a particular form or receive pictures, symbols, or images. A clairaudient may hear a "voice" or even music from the heavens. Angelic music is the most glorious music that you have ever heard. Perhaps a beautiful aroma may appear from nowhere – an exquisite gift from the heavens. "Feel" the presence of your guardian angel and breathe in all of its love.

8. Ask your guardian angel its name. Mentally or verbally, simply ask "What is your name?" and wait patiently for a reply. Listen to the voice of your angel in your heart and in your throat. Stay very much in touch with your feelings (our emotions are usually the first point of contact for our angels). If you do not receive an answer, do not worry: you

Count up to 10 as preparation for attuning to the angelic realm.

may receive a name next time. If the name was muffled, ask your guardian angel to speak louder and more clearly so that you can understand them.

9. Remain as long as you like in the company of your guardian angel. Breathe in the unconditional love flowing from your guardian angel and let it fill you with light and joy. Ask your angel to make you more conscious of the protection and guidance that is being given so graciously to you.

10. When you feel ready to return, thank your guardian angel for all of the guidance and blessings that you receive in your life.

11. Return to waking consciousness by counting slowly from ten to one. Tell yourself that when you awaken you will feel refreshed and full of love and radiance. You will be at peace and in harmony with life and will impart this serenity and unconditional love to others. Become aware of your body once again and feel your contact with the ground. Gently wriggle your fingers and toes. Notice your breathing. Slowly become aware of your surroundings and of all of the sounds and smells around you. Very gradually open your eyes.

At the end of the exercise, take a few minutes to record any messages or experiences as spontaneously as possible in your angel notebook. Do not try to change any words to make it look better: these words were given to you in this way by your guardian angel and are already perfect. They need no editing! You may be given words, pictures, symbols, or feelings. Accept whatever messages you have received with gratitude. Never dismiss any information or guidance that comes through to you.

It is common to feel very emotional and full of love and peace, for oneself and others, after an encounter with your guardian angel. If you do feel "moved," then your angel has undoubtedly communicated with you.

I hope that you have enjoyed your contact with your guardian angel and that this will be the first of many encounters for you!

Helping a Friend or Partner to Meet Their Angel

It is great fun to assist a friend or partner to commune with the angels. Perhaps your friend or partner has tried to contact the angels with no success and is feeling disheartened and fearful of farther disappointment. Maybe he or she does not "feel" spiritual enough or is even afraid of the angelic realms. With a little encouragement, he or she will be able to experience the joy of an angelic encounter. When two or more people come together to work with the angels it is a truly magical experience!

Preparation

Choose a time when you will be undisturbed and go to your angelic altar. Light a candle together, burn an incense stick, choose a spiritual essential oil, and put some fresh flowers on the altar to raise the vibrations of the room. As you prepare, try to keep conversation to a minimum and, if you do speak, keep your words very positive – angels are not attracted to idle gossip or negativity. They love peace, harmony, and joy.

Both of you should wear comfortable, loose-fitting clothes. You need to be able to move around your partner's (the receiver's) body freely and he or she does not want to feel constricted by a tight belt and so on. You will probably both find it comfortable, as well as grounding, to go barefoot.

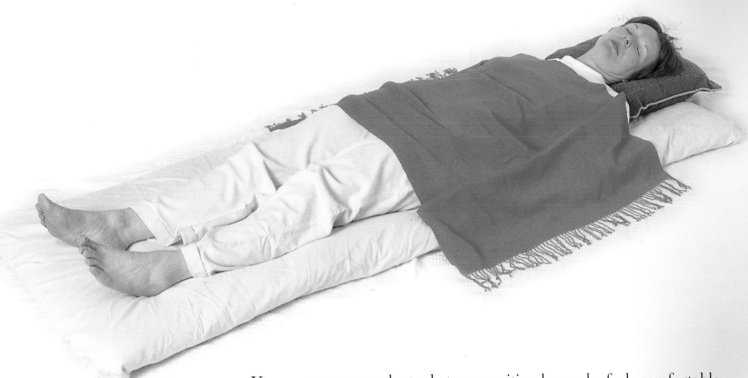

Your friend should lay or sit to receive the treatment – whichever they feel most comfortable with.

Your partner may adopt whatever position he or she feels comfortable with. You can carry out the treatment with the receiver lying on the floor on a well-padded surface, such as a comforter, one or two blankets, or a sleeping bag. Ask the receiver to lie on his or her back and place a pillow under their head and one under their knees. Cover them up with a blanket or towel, as their body temperature will drop as the treatment progresses. You will also need a pillow for you to kneel on while you administer the therapy.

Alternatively, the receiver may sit or kneel on some pillows on the floor. A stool is also acceptable, provided that the receiver's feet reach the floor. Ensure that their back is straight to establish a strong connection with the earth and to enable the angelic energies to flow freely.

Keep the lights as low as possible, or even turn them off completely and light a few more candles. A bright light shining into your partner's eyes is not conducive to relaxation!

Meeting the Guardian Angel

1. Kneel down beside your partner's feet. Close your eyes, breathe in, center yourself, and anchor yourself securely to the earth. Lower your hands gently onto your partner's feet and rest them there with a feather-light touch. Say to the receiver:

   Visualize tiny roots emerging from the soles of your feet and your spine, extending down into the center of the earth. These roots will ground you and will make you feel safe and secure.

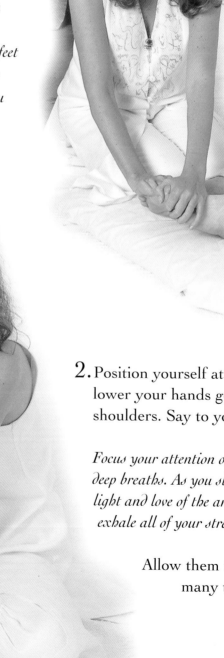

2. Position yourself at the receiver's head and lower your hands gently onto his or her shoulders. Say to your partner:

   Focus your attention on your breathing. Take a few deep breaths. As you slowly breathe in, inhale the light and love of the angels. As you breathe out, exhale all of your stress and tension.

   Allow them to inhale and exhale as many times as necessary.

3. Now say to him or her:

Focus your attention on your body. Travel down to your right foot and leg. Tighten the muscles here, then release, them letting all of the tension dissolve. Shift your attention to your left leg and foot — again tighten and then relax. Focus on your abdomen — tighten and release. Move up to the chest area — tighten and relax. Pull your shoulders forward and up toward your ears — release them. Make a fist with your right hand and lift your right arm slightly off the floor — let go and relax. Make a fist with your left hand and lift your left arm slightly off the floor — let go and relax. Move your neck gently and slowly from side to side — release your neck. Focus on your face — tighten up all of the muscles of your face and then let go. Scan your body from the top of your head down to your toes, releasing any remaining tension that you find.

Wait a minute or two for them to let go completely.

4. Place your hands gently on his or her head and say:

Visualize your entire body absorbing and filling up with the loving and protective light of the angels. Feel their beams of light flowing from the top of your head down to your feet, gently melting away any blockages. Rejoice in the radiance of their light.

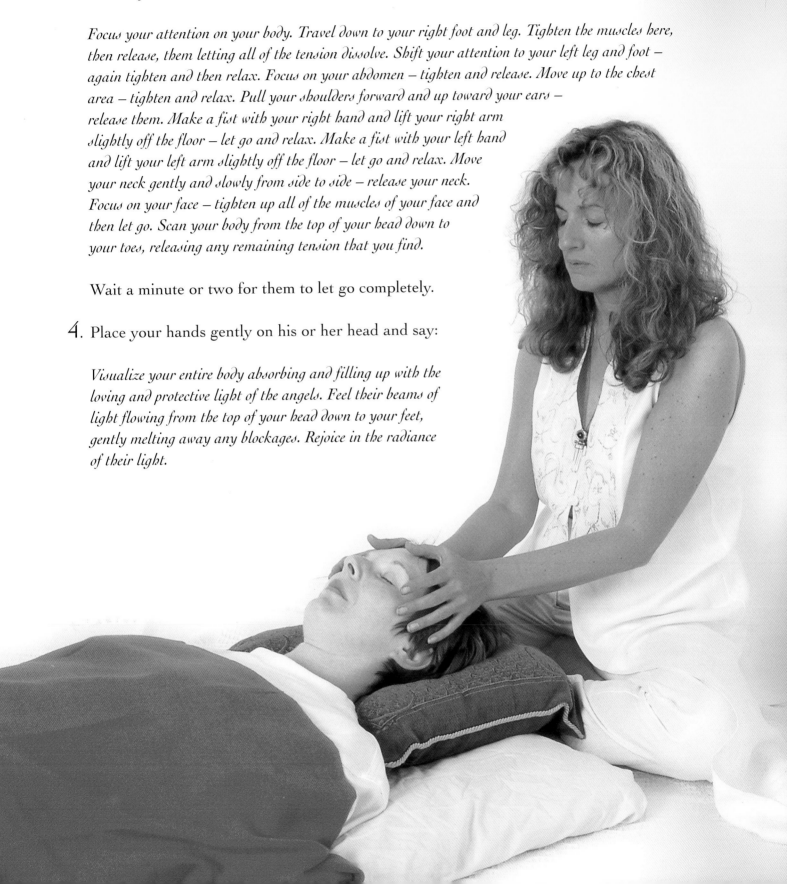

5. Gradually lower your hands so that they rest gently on the receiver's heart area and say:

Focus on your heart area and visualize it as an exquisite pink rose. Imagine this rose gradually opening, petal by petal, and filling with unconditional love. This is where your guardian angel will connect with you. Invite your angel into your heart.

Allow the receiver to attune to the presence of the guardian angel for a minute or so.

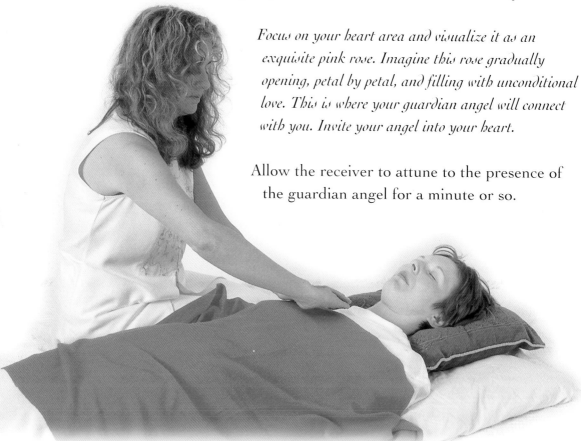

6. *Ask your guardian angel, either mentally or aloud:*
"What is your name?" Wait for a response.
Now ask your angel any questions you may have.

Allow the receiver a few minutes to receive any answers and to experience the love and light of the guardian angel.

7. *Now you are ready to return. Give thanks to your guardian angel for all of the guidance, love, and protection you receive every day of your life. I am now going to count very slowly from ten to one. By the time I reach one, you will be very aware of your physical body. Ten – nine – eight – seven – six – five – four – three – two – one.*

As you count, very gradually and slowly release your hands from the heart area.

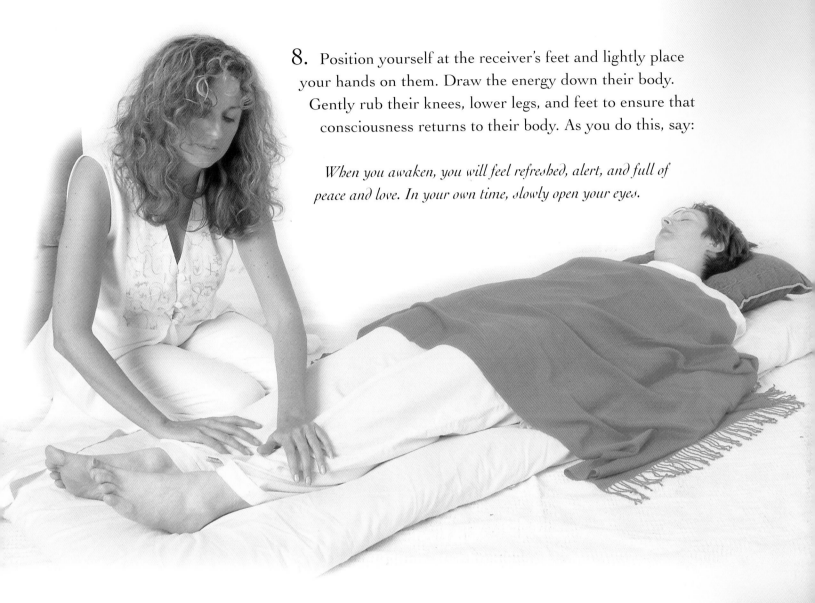

8. Position yourself at the receiver's feet and lightly place your hands on them. Draw the energy down their body. Gently rub their knees, lower legs, and feet to ensure that consciousness returns to their body. As you do this, say:

When you awaken, you will feel refreshed, alert, and full of peace and love. In your own time, slowly open your eyes.

On completion of the session, it is possible that your partner will be full of tears and inner peace – signs of angelic connection. You will both be flooded with unconditional love and overwhelming joy for the angels and will feel a strong connection between the two of you. Both of you will probably feel full of laughter, joy, and spontaneity and may want to giggle uncontrollably. Your senses may be heightened so that fragrances seem stronger and colors look sharper. You will now view the world as a place of wonder and delight. Ensure that you record any experiences in your angel notebook. Try to meet with your partner at least once a week to unite, connect, and work with your angels.

Angelic Essential Oils

Angelic Essential Oils

The use of fragrance is a very powerful tool for drawing angelic beings close to you. Aromas can open up and heighten our consciousness, making us more receptive to the heavenly hosts. Because of their purity, essential oils are particularly suitable for creating the vibration of love that is ideal for attracting angels. Oils produced under favorable conditions by loving and caring people that have not been adulterated and polluted will possess the perfect energy for spiritual use. I have already suggested that essential oils should form part of your angelic spiritual altar since the aromas raise the vibrations and invite the angels to approach us.

How to Use Essential Oils

There are several methods of using essential oils in your sacred space.

1. DIFFUSER

Put a few teaspoons of water in the bowl on top of the diffuser. Light the candle under the diffuser and then sprinkle a few drops of your chosen essential oil on to the water.

2. WATER BOWL

Fill a small bowl or saucer with boiling water and then add a few drops of essential oil. The steam will waft the heavenly smelling aroma around the room.

3. CANDLES

Light a candle to allow a small amount of wax to melt. Blow out the candle and add three drops of essential oil to the melted wax. Take care not to drop any oil on the wick as essential oils are highly flammable. Now carefully light the candle once more.

4. ROOM SPRAYS

Fill a small plant spray with water and add ten drops of essential oil. Spray your spiritual haven, but take care to avoid polished surfaces.

5. PILLOWS

Sprinkle two drops of essential oil on the pillows in the sacred space that you use for meditation, therapy, and angelic exercises. At night, put two drops on your pillow to encourage communication with your angels during your dreamtime. Alternatively, put the drops on absorbent-cotton balls and place them inside your pillowcases.

6. INCENSE OR SMUDGE STICKS

Add three drops of essential oil to incense sticks and smudge sticks.

7. HANDS

Put one drop of essential oil on to the palm of one of your hands. Rub both palms together and hold your hands in the prayer position, close to your face.

The essential oils with which you choose to contact the spiritual realms are very much a matter of personal choice. It will depend on where you are on your spiritual journey and which angels you are trying to contact. Choose aromas that resonate and harmonize with you to facilitate angelic connections.

As I have previously mentioned, angels have their own particular "fragrances." Very often, just prior to an angelic appearance, an exquisite aroma that is not of this world will suddenly fill the room. These heavenly aromas are indescribably beautiful and haunting and often linger long after the angel has departed.

Blending Essential Oils

While creating a spiritual blend of essential oils, ensure that your mind is completely free of all earthly thoughts. Radiate love and peace as you mix the oils, and this will be transmitted into the blend.

I have been guided by the angelic realms intuitively to develop my own special archangel blends that resonate exceptionally well with the archangels that I have assigned them to. I use them for anointing and wear them as a perfume whenever I wish to draw a particular archangel close to me.

Why not create your own special fragrances? Simply add one or two drops of essential oil per teaspoon (five milliliters) of sweet almond or jojoba oil. If you wish to mix a blend and keep it for future use, you will need to put it into an amber-colored bottle or you will lose, or at least diminish, the spiritual, as well as the therapeutic effects, of the blend. To a thirty milliliter, amber-colored bottle, add nine drops in total of your chosen angelic essential oils. This blend will keep its potency for approximately three months.

What follows is an outline of the essential oils, all of which will enable you to connect with your angels.

Angelica seed
(Angelica archangelica)

Aroma Clear, sharp, fresh.
Spiritual uses As its name suggests, angelica seed has a strong affinity with the angelic realms. It enables us to create heaven on earth. Angelica is ideal for use on sceptical and spiritually bereft individuals who feel that they have no connection with, or have lost their links to, the heavenly hosts. It helps to open up the intuition and to put us more in touch with our higher self.

Blends well with Bergamot, carrot seed, clary sage, geranium, jasmine, rose, sandalwood.
Special precautions Avoid during pregnancy.

Benzoin
(Styrax benzoin)

Aroma Vanillalike.
Spiritual uses Benzoin assists us in opening up the heart chakra, which is essential if we are to connect with the angels. It is a protective oil that encourages our guardian angels and the angels of protection to draw closer. It resonates with the Archangel Michael. Benzoin also helps us to feel "grounded" and safe.

Blends well with Bergamot, frankincense, geranium, jasmine, patchouli, palmarosa, rose, sandalwood, vetivert.
Special precautions None.

Bergamot
(Citrus bergamia)

Aroma Light, fresh, citrus.
Spiritual uses Bergamot possesses a very high spiritual vibration that allows us to become quickly attuned to the spiritual realms. It helps to lift the thin veil that separates us from the angelic kingdom. Bergamot draws the angels of joy and illumination closer to us. It resonates with the Archangel Jophiel.

Blends well with All essential oils, particularly clary sage, geranium, jasmine, lavender, mandarin, melissa, neroli, sandalwood, ylang ylang.
Special precautions Do not apply prior to sunbathing as it increases the photosensitivity of the skin.

Black pepper
(Piper nigrum)

Aroma Sharp, spicy, hot, warming.
Spiritual uses An excellent oil to assist those who have become "stuck" on their spiritual pathway and feel lethargic and unable to communicate with the angels. It also helps to instill courage and breaks down any fears of connecting with the angelic realms. Black pepper attracts the angels of strength and guidance.

Blends well with Basil, bergamot, carrot seed, coriander, cypress, fennel, frankincense, geranium, ginger, grapefruit, juniper, lemon, lemongrass, lime, mandarin, myrrh, orange, palmarosa, rosemary, rosewood, sage, sandalwood, ylang ylang.
Special precautions None.

Carrot seed
(Daucus carota)

Aroma Sharp, pungent.
Spiritual uses Useful for opening up our "third eye" and giving us visions and insight. It enables us to see our angels more clearly and to receive the angelic messages with insight and clarity.

Blends well with Angelica seed, basil, black pepper, cajeput, cardamon, cinnamon, coriander, fennel, ginger, juniper, lemon, lime, mandarin, orange, palmarosa, rosemary, rosewood.
Special precautions None.

Cedarwood (Atlas)
(Cedrus atlantica)

Aroma Warm, woody, heady.
Spiritual uses Cedarwood brings the angels of purification closer to us. They assist in purifying us of physical and emotional blockages, which prevent us from receiving the wisdom and harmony of the angels. The more we release them, the more we will raise our vibrations, making it easier to open up to the angels.

Blends well with Bergamot, cardamon, chamomile, cypress, frankincense, geranium, grapefruit, juniper, lemon, lime, neroli, orange, palmarosa, petitgrain, pine, rosemary, rosewood, yarrow.
Special precautions 1. Avoid when pregnant.
2. Do not use on babies and young children.

Chamomile (Roman)
(Anthemis nobilis)

Aroma Warm, sweet, floral, aromatic.
Spiritual uses Chamomile connects us with our inner child and gently brings healing, forgiveness, and comfort. It is particularly indicated for children and helps to establish and strengthen the love between parents and their children. Chamomile enables us to let go of our anger and restlessness, bringing peace to a troubled spirit. This oil will draw the angels of children and the angels of peace closer to us.

Blends well with Benzoin, bergamot, geranium, immortelle, mandarin, neroli, jasmine, palmarosa, rose, yarrow.
Special precautions None. Ideal for babies and young children.

Clary sage
(Salvia sclarea)

Aroma Sweet, heady, floral.
Spiritual uses A wonderful oil for opening us up to the angels. Excellent for those who are overly physical and find it difficult, or are too fearful, to open up the consciousness to the possibility of spiritual realms. Clary sage helps us to deal with inner conflicts and brings peace and harmony to a troubled soul.

Blends well with Angelica seed, bergamot, chamomile, cedarwood, frankincense, geranium, jasmine, lavender, linden blossom, neroli, rose, rosewood, sandalwood, ylang ylang.
Special precautions Do not take large doses together with alcohol as this may induce a narcotic effect.

Clove bud
(Eugenia caryophyllata)

Aroma Rich, spicy, strong, warm.
Spiritual uses Clove assists in the awakening of our senses and urges us forward on our soul pathway. For those who feel unfulfilled, stuck in a rut, "lost," confused, and uncertain as to their spirituality, clove helps to spark a deeper understanding of the self. It brings forth the angels of insight.

Blends well with Angelica seed, basil, benzoin, black pepper, cypress, frankincense, ginger, lavender, lemon, mandarin, orange, palmarosa, rosemary, rosewood.
Special precautions
1. Avoid during pregnancy.
2. Take care with sensitive skin.
3. Do not use on babies and children.

Cypress
(Cupressus sempivirens)

Aroma Woody, balsamic.
Spiritual uses Cypress draws the angels of transition and the angels of comfort to us. It is particularly useful when someone is dying to ease the passing of the soul into the next world. It gives strength to those who are recently bereaved. Cypress may be used to help us to move through any changes that may be happening in our lives.

Blends well with Benzoin, bergamot, cedarwood, frankincense, juniper, lemon, lime, pine, rose, rosewood, rosemary.
Special precautions None.

Dill seed
(Anethum graveolens)

Aroma Sweet, herbaceous.
Spiritual uses Dill encourages the assistance of the angels of harmony. It is particularly useful for those whose inner conflicts have resulted in eating disorders. Dill calms, soothes, and heals the solar plexus and the digestive system. The fragrance of dill elevates us so that the heavenly realms may nourish us.

Blends well with Angelica seed, coriander, cardamon, carrot seed, chamomile, fennel, ginger, lemon, lime, mandarin, peppermint, spearmint.
Special precautions None.

Elemi
(Canarium luzonicum)

Aroma Fresh, spicy, citrus.
Spiritual uses Elemi is a very spiritual oil that facilitates a deeper connection with the angels of peace and the divine. It opens up the heart, revealing the inner being. Elemi can also provide a warm cloak of comfort when our spirits are low and we need protection. Elemi encourages stillness, peace, contentment, and calm.

Blends well with Benzoin, cedarwood, chamomile, frankincense, jasmine, linden blossom, marjoram, myrrh, patchouli, rosewood, sandalwood.
Special precautions None.

Fennel (sweet)
(Foeniculum vulgare)

Aroma Aniseedlike, strong.
Spiritual uses Fennel brings the light of the angels of courage, strength, and hope toward us. It gives us the strength to face difficult situations and to move on in the face of seemingly impossible hurdles. Fennel clears the body, mind, and spirit of toxins and fills us with energy and vigor so that we may have the strength to take on new tasks.

Blends well with Bergamot, black pepper, cardamon, coriander, cypress, dill, ginger, juniper, lemon, lime, mandarin, peppermint, spearmint, rosemary.
Special precautions 1. Do not use bitter fennel.
2. Avoid excessive use on babies and children.
3. Avoid use on epileptics.
4. Avoid during pregnancy.

Frankincense
(Boswellia carterii)

Aroma Woody, balsamic, spicy, warming.
Spiritual uses An oil from the heavens that helps us to achieve a heightened state of spiritual awareness in which to commune with our angels. The ancient wisdom of frankincense enables us to unlock the keys of the universe. Frankincense helps us to move on spiritually and enables us to allow the spirit to step in and out of the body, knowing that we are safe and protected.

Blends well with Benzoin, cedarwood, cypress, elemi, jasmine, linden blossom, myrrh, patchouli, rose, rosewood, sandalwood, vetivert.
Special precautions None.

Geranium
(Pelargonium graveolens)

Aroma Sweet, roselike.
Spiritual uses Geranium brings us closer to the angels of peace and the angels of love. It balances the emotions, dispelling anxiety and nervous tension and lifting depression. Geranium possesses a very feminine energy and connects us with the angels of reproduction and birth. It may help infertility.

Blends well with Bergamot, chamomile, clary sage, cypress, jasmine, lemon, mandarin, melissa, neroli, rose, sandalwood, ylang ylang.
Special precautions None.

Ginger
(Zingiber officinale)

Aroma Aromatic, hot, spicy.
Spiritual uses Ginger carries an aroma that is full of fire, courage, and protection. It resonates with the Archangel Michael to give us the fearlessness to face any obstacle, no matter how great. Ginger stimulates us into divine action. It helps us to see through the illusions of everyday life and lifts the veil between us and the angelic realms.

Blends well with Bergamot, black pepper, coriander, grapefruit, juniper, lemon, lime, orange, palmarosa, rosemary, rosewood, vetivert.
Special precautions Take care with sensitive skin.

Grapefruit
(Citrus paradisi)

Aroma Fresh, sweet, refreshing.
Spiritual uses Grapefruit opens up our hearts to the angelic realms and brings the angelic messengers of joy close to us. It uplifts us, inducing a sense of euphoria, and transmutes any negativity. Grapefruit helps to restore our inner light and clears any blockages to the divine.

Blends well with Cypress, cedarwood, clary sage, geranium, ginger, jasmine, mandarin, melissa, myrtle, neroli, rose, rosewood.
Special precautions Take care with hypersensitive skin.

Hyssop
(Hyssopus officinalis)

Aroma Strong, herbal, camphorlike.
Spiritual uses Hyssop helps to purify the body, mind, and spirit. It removes feelings of uncleanliness, for instance, after someone has been raped or sexually, physically, or psychically attacked. Those who have negative feelings about themselves can be helped by the angels of purification, who will remove the guilt and fear commonly experienced after an assault.

Blends well with Bergamot, cedarwood, cypress, frankincense, grapefruit, juniper, marjoram, myrrh, rosemary, rosewood.
Special precautions
1. Avoid during pregnancy.
2. Do not use on epileptics.
3. Avoid in cases of high blood pressure.
4. Do not use on babies and children.

Immortelle (everlasting)
(Helichrysum augustifolium)

Aroma Powerful, rich.
Spiritual uses Immortelle dispels any spiritual apprehension and instills in us a belief in the divine. It gives us the insight into a life after death – we are everlasting. Immortelle is ideal for those who are deeply wounded and feel it difficult to connect with their angels. The unconditional love of Archangel Chamuel is called for here to heal the hurt.

Blends well with Bergamot, cedarwood, chamomile, clary sage, cypress, geranium, jasmine, mandarin, myrtle, neroli, palmarosa, rose, rosewood, vetivert, ylang ylang.
Special precautions None.

Jasmine
(Jasminum officinale)

Aroma Exotic, floral, heady, sensual.
Spiritual uses An exquisite aroma sent from the heavens, jasmine opens up our consciousness to the angels of love, compassion, and forgiveness. A wonderful oil for lifting sadness and inducing optimism and confidence. Jasmine is favored by the angels and is guaranteed to draw in a whole host of heavenly beings.

Blends well with Benzoin, bergamot, geranium, lemon, mandarin, myrtle, neroli, petitgrain, rose, rosewood, sandalwood, ylang ylang.
Special precautions None.

Juniper
(Juniperus communis)

Aroma Fresh, woody.
Spiritual uses The supreme cleanser of body, mind, and spirit, juniper attracts the angels of purification. It is a classic remedy for clearing away past traumas and karma and reminds us not to keep on repeating the same mistakes. Juniper also calls forth the angels of protection, who will not allow any harmful influences to pass through their shields.

Blends well with Bergamot, cypress, fennel, frankincense, geranium, lemon, mandarin, myrtle, pine, vetivert, yarrow.
Special precautions 1. Avoid during pregnancy.
2. Avoid using excessively if there is inflammation of the kidneys.

Lavender
(Lavendula augustifolia)

Aroma Sweet, floral.
Spiritual uses Lavender brings the angels of harmony and balance closer to us. It restores "wholeness," bringing us back into a state of true equilibrium. Lavender assists in regenerating not only areas of the physical body that are torn, but also helps to repair any auric damage. It is full of love and compassion and will bring you great comfort and solace in times of distress.

Blends well with Bergamot, chamomile, clary sage, cypress, frankincense, geranium, grapefruit, jasmine, lemon, lime, neroli, palmarosa, petitgrain, rose, sandalwood, ylang ylang.
Special precautions None.

Lemon
(Citrus limonum)

Aroma Clean, crisp, fruity, refreshing.
Spiritual uses Lemon cleanses body, mind, and spirit and draws the angels of purification close to us. It also carries with it the strength and the power of the Archangel Michael. Lemon helps to restore strength and vitality to a depleted spirit, reestablishing faith in the divine.

Blends well with Bergamot, black pepper, cypress, fennel, frankincense, geranium, grapefruit, ginger, hyssop, juniper, lime, mandarin, rosemary, rosewood, thyme.
Special precautions Avoid strong sunlight immediately after treatment.

Linden blossom
(Tilia caudata)

Aroma Exquisite, heady, floral, sweet.
Spiritual uses Linden blossom is one of the primary angelic oils – it has such a heavenly scent. It will draw you to the angels of peace, love, forgiveness, and healing. Linden blossom has a strong affinity for the heart, replacing sadness with joy. This angelic aroma is ideal for those who have either never experienced true love or have been badly treated in love. Its exquisite fragrance will open up our consciousness and connect us with the heavens.

Blends well with Benzoin, clary sage, frankincense, geranium, jasmine, lemon, mandarin, neroli, petitgrain, palmarosa, rose, sandalwood, ylang ylang.
Special precautions None.

Mandarin
(Citrus reticulata)

Aroma Sweet, floral, fruity.
Spiritual uses Mandarin is the favorite oil of the angels of joy. It encourages feelings of happiness and contentment and urges us to play like children. Whenever you feel down, take out the essential oil of mandarin and connect with your angels of joy and you will be full of uncontrollable laughter within no time. An excellent oil for children.

Blends well with Bergamot, geranium, jasmine, myrtle, neroli, palmarosa, petitgrain, rose, rosewood, spearmint.
Special precautions Avoid strong sunlight immediately after treatment.

Marjoram (sweet)
(Origanum marjorana)

Aroma Sweet, warming.
Spiritual uses Marjoram is indicated for restless, tormented souls who can find no peace in this world. They live in a constant state of agitation – physical, emotional, mental, and psychic. This oil resonates with Archangel Raphael and his team of healing angels, who will descend to deal with the inner conflicts and torment and create peace and harmony. It is a warming, protective essential oil that also attratcts Archangel Michael.

Blends well with Benzoin, cedarwood, chamomile, clary sage, cypress, geranium, jasmine, lavender, linden blossom, neroli, rose, sandalwood, ylang ylang.
Special precautions Avoid during pregnancy.

Melissa (true)
(Melissa officinalis)

Aroma Sweet, fresh, lemony,
Spiritual uses A very spiritual oil that is a favorite fragrance of the angelic realms. Melissa quickly draws beings of light toward us, filling our hearts with joy. Melissa is extremely uplifting on a spiritual level and acts as a bridge between heaven and earth. It enables us to connect with the angels of prophecy during meditation and will bring visions.

Blends well with Angelica seed, benzoin, cedarwood, chamomile, frankincense, geranium, linden blossom, neroli, rose, rosewood.
Special precautions Melissa is often sold in a blended form as it is a very expensive oil. Therefore take care with sensitive skins.

Myrrh
(Commiphora myrrha)

Aroma Warm, balsamic, musty.
Spiritual uses Myrrh is for those souls who are deeply wounded by their traumatic experiences in both this life and past lives. It resonates with the angels of karma, who will encourage such troubled spirits to let go and move on in this life. Myrrh is excellent for individuals who find it hard to speak up for themselves. It draws the angels of communication closer to us so that we may stand up for ourselves and express what we really feel.

Blends well with Bergamot, chamomile, cypress, frankincense, grapefruit, hyssop, immortelle, lemon, mandarin, myrtle, palmarosa, patchouli, yarrow.
Special precautions Avoid during pregnancy.

Myrtle
(Myrtus communis)

Aroma Sweet, herbaceous.
Spiritual uses In the 16th century, myrtle was a major ingredient of "angel water." It will draw the Archangel Chamuel and angels of love close to our hearts so that we are filled with blessings from the divine. An oil of purity that encourages unconditional love, both for ourselves and others, myrtle is useful when there are relationship problems. It helps to heal rifts and gently supports us in moments of distress. Myrtle also encourages forgiveness.

Blends well with Angelica seed, benzoin, bergamot, elemi, geranium, immortelle, lemon, linden blossom, mandarin, rose, violet leaf, yarrow.
Special precautions None.

Neroli
(Citrus aurantium)

Aroma Fresh, floral, haunting.
Spiritual uses Neroli possesses a very high vibration and its aroma will send us soaring into the angelic realms. It has the ability to fill our body, mind, and spirit with light. Neroli helps to spark a deeper understanding of the self and can awaken those who are "sleeping" and unaware of their spirituality. It can also help those souls who repeatedly make the same mistakes and have difficulties in finding answers and moving forward in life.

Blends well with Bergamot, chamomile, frankincense, geranium, grapefruit, jasmine, linden blossom, mandarin, myrtle, orange, rose, sandalwood, ylang ylang.
Special precautions None.

Palmarosa
(Cymbopogan martinii)

Aroma Sweet, rosy.
Spiritual uses The sweet fragrance of palmarosa draws the angels of love and beauty close to our hearts, bestowing happiness and joy upon us. Palmarosa lifts those souls who have been mistreated or neglected and have had their confidence undermined. Its aroma gently boosts our self-esteem, making us aware of our true worth.

Blends well with Benzoin, chamomile, frankincense, geranium, grapefruit, jasmine, lemon, lemongrass, mandarin, melissa, neroli, sandalwood, rose.
Special precautions None.

Patchouli
(Pogostemon patchouli)

Aroma Sweet, earthy, musty.
Spiritual uses Patchouli connects us with the angels of the earth. An excellent oil for those who feel ungrounded and find it difficult to function well in the physical world. Patchouli helps to establish a secure link between heaven and earth. It can gently ease us back to our earthly home and give us the realization that this incarnation is simply one small part of life's long journey.

Blends well with Benzoin, bergamot, elemi, frankincense, grapefruit, jasmine, lime, mandarin, neroli, orange, rose, sandalwood, vetivert.
Special precautions None.

Pine (Scots)
(Pinus sylvestris)

Aroma Clean, fresh, forestlike, penetrating.
Spiritual uses The powerful fragrance of pine awakens those who are "sleeping" and enlightens the self to its inner wisdom. Pine can bring us brilliant flashes of insight and resonates with the angels of creativity and illumination. An excellent oil to use if we feel surrounded by negative influences – it will help drive them away. Pine is also associated with endurance and perseverance and is ideal for those who feel fatigued, debilitated, and unable to cope.

Blends well with Basil, cedarwood, cypress, eucalyptus, frankincense, juniper, marjoram, peppermint, rosemary, rosewood.
Special precautions Do not use on sensitive skin.

Ravensara
(Ravensara aromatica)

Aroma Strong, medicinal, penetrating.
Spiritual uses Ravensara draws the angels of communication closer. Its fragrance has an affinity for the throat chakra, which becomes blocked if a person is not expressing his or her true desires. Ravensara encourages us to be who we really are. It puts us back on our soul pathway and transmits courage and fearlessness. Ravensara heralds the arrival of Archangel Michael and his army of powerful angels, who will give us the courage

to be true to ourselves and not to give in to the demands of other people.
Blends well with Black pepper, cypress, elemi, frankincense, ginger, hyssop, immortelle, juniper, lemon, myrrh, myrtle, niaouli, pine, rosewood, thyme.
Special precautions None.

Rose
(Rosa damascena, Rosa centifolia)

Aroma Sweet, heady, intoxicating, heavenly.
Spiritual uses The heavenly fragrance of rose immediately transports us to the etheric realms. Rose Otto aligns our consciousness with the angels of love, beauty, and forgiveness and touches the very depths of the soul. The aroma has a profound effect on the heart, alleviating sorrow, bitterness, and resentment and awakening love and compassion. As we breathe in the fragrance of rose, we draw in the pure love of the angels.

Blends well with Benzoin, bergamot, chamomile, geranium, grapefruit, jasmine, lemon, lime, linden blossom, mandarin, neroli, petitgrain, sandalwood, ylang ylang.
Special precautions None.

Rosemary
(Rosmarinus officinalis)

Aroma Clean, strong, camphoraceous.
Spiritual uses Rosemary is the oil of "remembrance" that helps us to find answers to our questions. It brings forth information and understanding about our past lives, sheds light on the purpose of our role on earth, and clears away confusion. An excellent oil for those who have "lost" their spirit. It helps us to reconnect with our guides and angels. Rosemary also provides us with a shield of protection and calls forth the power of the Archangel Michael.

Blends well with Basil, black pepper, cedarwood, clove, coriander, eucalyptus, ginger, myrtle, naouli, peppermint, ravensara, rosewood, sage, thyme.
Special precautions
1. Avoid during the first stages of pregnancy.
2. Do not use extensively on epileptics.

Rosewood
(Aniba rosaeodora)

Aroma Sweet, floral, woody.
Spiritual uses The mystical fragrance of rosewood is an excellent aid for meditation and enables us to open the door to the spiritual realms. It establishes a clear pathway for communication with our angels and encourages the gift of prophecy. When we are uncertain, rosewood clears away the confusion and shows us the way forward. Rosewood balances and enlivens all of the chakras.

Blends well with Basil, cedarwood, chamomile, elemi, hyssop, linden blossom, myrtle, palmarosa, petitgrain, pine, ravensara, rosemary.
Special precautions None.

Sage
(Salvia offinalis)

Aroma Camphoraceous, herbaceous, warm.
Spiritual uses The powerful fragrance of sage summons the angels of protection and purification to our side. It can be used to purify the environment, to cleanse the aura of unwanted thoughts and emotions, and to protect us from the forces of darkness. It has the power to transform darkness into light. Sage carries with it the wisdom of the ages and can unveil the secrets of the universe.

Blends well with Benzoin, cedarwood, elemi, frankincense, hyssop, myrrh, myrtle, patchouli, rose, rosewood, vetivert, violet leaf, yarrow.
Special precautions 1. Avoid during pregnancy.
2. Avoid when breast-feeding.
3. Do not use on babies and children.
4. Do not use extensively on individuals with epilepsy.
5. Do not use extensively on individuals with high blood pressure.

Sandalwood
(Santalum album)

Aroma Sweet, warm, woody, lingering.
Spiritual uses A bridge between heaven and earth, the fragrance of sandalwood sends us soaring from the physical into the spiritual realms. It has an affinity with the angels of love and forgiveness. Where there is no forgiveness, negative emotions, such as anger, fear, guilt, and resentment, may arise. Sandalwood embodies love and forgiveness and helps one to forgive oneself and others, thus dispelling dense, negative energies. This heavenly fragrance also calls forth the angels of peace, who bring tranquility and stillness to restless, troubled souls.

Blends well with Benzoin, bergamot, clary sage, frankincense, geranium, jasmine, melissa, neroli, palmarosa, petitgrain, rose, ylang ylang.
Special precautions None.

Vetivert
(Vetivera zizanioides)

Aroma Earthy, smoky, woody.
Spiritual uses Vetivert is the perfect oil for those who feel spiritually ungrounded. The distinctive aroma connects us with the angels of the earth and gives us the strength and courage to be in the physical world and work through the often difficult lessons of life that are put before us. Vetivert is the oil of tranquility that can stop the persistent thoughts that go round in the mind and can put everything into perspective, bringing the whole being back into balance.

The fragrance of vetivert also brings protection and purifies and strengthens the aura.
Blends well with Bergamot, clary sage, geranium, jasmine, juniper, lemon, lemongrass, mandarin, neroli, petitgrain, sage, sandalwood, yarrow.
Special precautions None.

Yarrow
(Achillea millefolium)

Aroma Strong, medicinal.
Spiritual uses This fragrance allows us to access the angelic realms while at the same time protecting and nurturing us. A wonderful oil for attuning us to the spiritual self under the safety of the wings of the angels of protection. Yarrow is an excellent oil to use whilst traveling to other dimensions and unlocking the secrets of the universe. It also has the ability to bring a "monkey mind" into a deep, meditative state to enable us to commune with our inner being to become at one with the divine. Yarrow also brings forth prophecies and visions.

Blends well with Chamomile, elemi, frankincense, immortelle, myrrh, neroli, myrtle, patchouli, sage, sandalwood, vetivert, ylang ylang.
Special precautions 1. Take care during pregnancy.
2. Do not use on babies and children.

Ylang ylang
(Canaga odorata)

Aroma Exotic, heady, sweet.
Spiritual uses The fragrance of ylang ylang releases us from the anguish of mental turmoil. It shuts down the troubles and unanswerable questions that can plague the mind. It gently calms inner disquiet and, in the stillness, calls forth the answers that we seek. Ylang ylang gently opens up the heart and heals the wounds that can deter us from entering into relationships. It draws the angels of forgiveness to our hearts so that we may once again love ourselves and others. The angels teach us that divine love embraces us all.

Blends well with Bergamot, chamomile, geranium, grapefruit, jasmine, lemon, mandarin, neroli, orange, patchouli, palmarosa, rose, sandalwood.
Special precautions None.

Angels and the Chakras

As you connect with your angels, you become much more aware of your nonphysical self.

Apart from the physical body, we also have an energy field that completely surrounds us that is known as the "aura." On religious paintings of angels and saints, the aura can often be seen depicted as a halo.

We also have energy centers, known as "chakras," that pick up the universal life force and distribute it throughout the body. The word *chakra* is a Sanskrit word that literally means "wheel," "disk," or "circle." A chakra is a vortex, a constantly revolving wheel of energy. There are seven major chakras, or "master" chakras, that run in a line through the body, from the base of the spine to the top of the head. There are also many minor chakras.

I will now briefly describe each chakra. I will then explain how to sense the chakras and to connect the angels and archangels with these energy centers for healing.

The Seven Major Chakras

FIRST CHAKRA

Name: base/root

Sanskrit name: Muladhara

Location: base of the spine in the perineum, between the anus and the genitals

Color: red

Petals: four

Element: earth

Associated glands: adrenals, some say the gonads (i.e., ovaries, testes)

Function:

- **Mental/emotional**
  Survival
  Security
  Grounding
  Support
- **Physical**
  Lower digestive tract
- **Psychic**
  Spatial intuition

Angelic oils: benzoin, patchouli, vetivert

Angels/archangels: Archangel Sandalphon, angels of the earth

Crystals: red stones: garnet, red calcite, red jasper, ruby

black stones: black tourmaline, obsidian, smoky quartz

SECOND CHAKRA

Name: abdomen/sacral/sexual

Sanskrit name: Svadhisthana

Location: lower abdomen, just below the navel

Color: orange

Petals: six

Element: water

Associated glands: gonads (i.e., ovaries, testes), some say the spleen

Function:

- **Mental/emotional**
  Sensuality
  Intimacy
  Creativity
  Possession

- **Physical**
  Sexual organs
  Kidney
  Bladder
  Prostate
- **Psychic**
  Clairsentience

Angelic oils: carrot seed, dill, geranium, hyssop, jasmine, marjoram, neroli, rose, sandalwood

Angels/archangels: Archangel Chamuel (relationships), angels of birth, Archangel Gabriel

Crystals: amber, carnelian, citrine, golden labradorite (orange sunstone), orange calcite, topaz

THIRD CHAKRA

Name: solar plexus

Sanskrit name: Manipura

Location: between the umbilicus (navel) and the solar plexus

Color: yellow

Petals: ten

Element: fire

Associated glands: pancreas, some say the adrenals

Function:

- **Mental/emotional**
  Power
  Accomplishments
  Confidence
  Self-esteem
  Courage
  Emotional stability

- **Physical**
  Upper digestive tract
  Control of insulin
  Control of food intake
- **Psychic**
  Sensitivity to "vibes"

Angelic oils: benzoin, bergamot, black pepper, chamomile, clary sage, cypress, dill, elemi, fennel, hyssop, juniper, lemon, marjoram, neroli, palmarosa, sage

Angels/archangels: Archangel Uriel, angels of peace, Archangel Michael, Archangel Jophiel

Crystals: citrine, golden sunstone, tiger's eye, yellow jasper

FOURTH CHAKRA

Name: heart

Sanskrit name: Anahata

Location: center of the chest

Color: green (pink)

Petals: twelve

Element: air

Associated gland: thymus

Function:

- **Mental/emotional**
  Unconditional love
  Compassion
- **Physical**
  Heart and circulation
  Respiratory system
  Immune system
- **Psychic**
  Empathy

Angelic oils: benzoin, bergamot, cinnamon, clove, elemi, geranium, grapefruit, immortelle, lavender, lime, linden blossom, mandarin, neroli, palmarosa, rose, sandalwood

Angels/archangels: Archangel Chamuel, Archangel Raphael (healing)

Crystals: aventurine, chrysoprase, emerald, jade, kunzite, rose quartz

FIFTH CHAKRA

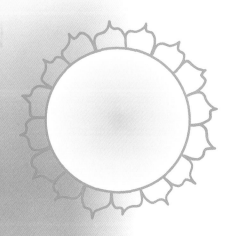

Name: throat

Sanskrit name: Visshuda

Location: throat

Color: blue

Petals: sixteen

Element: sound/ether

Associated gland: thyroid

Function:

- **Mental/emotional**
  Communication
  Expression
  Speaking and hearing the truth
  Spontaneity
- **Physical**
  Throat
  Vocal cords
  Ears
  Neck and shoulders
- **Psychic**
  Clairaudience

Angelic oils: black pepper, blue chamomile, cajeput, cypress, elemi, eucalyptus, myrrh, palmarosa, ravensara, rosemary, sage, yarrow

Angels/archangels: Archangel Michael

Crystals: aquamarine, blue calcite, blue lace agate, chrysocolla, lapis lazuli, turquoise

SIXTH CHAKRA

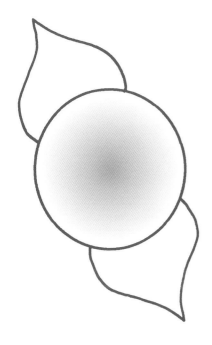

Name: third eye/brow

Sanskrit name: Ajna

Location: center of the forehead

Color: indigo

Petals: two (the two physical eyes surrounding the third eye), some say ninety-six (two times forty-eight)

Element: light

Associated glands: pituitary, some say pineal

Function:

- **Mental/emotional**
  Intuition
  Clarity
  Vision
  Discernment

- **Physical**
  Pituitary gland
  Eyes
- **Psychic**
  Clairvoyance

Angelic oils: angelica seed, basil, black pepper, carrot seed, clary sage, clove bud, ginger, melissa (true), peppermint, pine, rosemary, rosewood

Angels/archangels: Archangel Gabriel, Archangel Jophiel

Crystals: blue calcite, iolite, lapis lazuli, tanzanite

SEVENTH CHAKRA

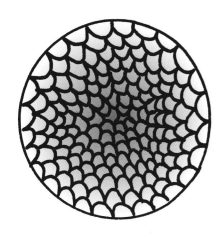

Name: crown

Sanskrit name: Sahasrara

Location: top of the head (anterior fontanelle of newborn babies)

Color: violet

Petals: one thousand

Element: thought/knowing

Associated glands: pineal, some say pituitary

Function:

- **Mental/emotional**
  Spirituality
  Link with higher self

- **Physical**
  Pineal gland
  Brain, mind
- **Psychic**
  Cognizance (inner knowledge)
  Cosmic consciousness

Angelic oils: cedarwood, elemi, frankincense, jasmine, linden blossom, neroli, rose, rosewood, violet leaf

Angels/archangels: Archangel Zadkiel

Crystals: amethyst, charoite, clear quartz, selenite

Sensing the Chakras With a Partner

Preparation

Choose a time when you will be undisturbed and then enter the sacred space that you have created. Ensure that both of you are wearing comfortable clothes and perform a simple opening ritual together to farther raise the vibrations, such as lighting a candle or a stick of incense or choosing an essential oil.

Ask your partner (the receiver) to lie down, either on their front or back, on a comfortable, well-padded surface with pillows under their head and knees. You may cover them up with a blanket or towel. You will need a pillow to kneel on while you are sensing the chakras. Alternatively, the receiver may sit on the floor or on a stool, provided that their feet touch the floor so that they are properly grounded.

Sensing

1. Kneel down by the side of the receiver. Close your eyes and focus on your body and breathing. Ground yourself, visualizing roots extending from your spine and penetrating deep into the earth.

2. Ask the receiver to take a few deep breaths. Inhale the light of the angels and exhale any stress and tension.

3. Rub your hands briskly together until your palms feel warm. Gently lower your hands until they are hovering just a few inches above the receiver's body at the base of the spine. This is the **root chakra**. Try to sense the energy of the chakra radiating toward the palms of your hands. Experiment with just using your right hand, your left hand, and then both hands, one on top of the other. Also try varying the distance from your hands to the receiver's body. There is no right or wrong way to sense the energy centers – find your most receptive position. Notice any sensations in your hands – heat, coldness, tingling, excess, or lack of, energy.

4. Once you have experienced the energy of the root chakra, move your hands up the receiver's body slightly to the **sacral chakra**, which is located just below the navel. Feel the energy of this chakra.

5. Move up the receiver's body and continue your sensing over the **solar-plexus chakra** (above the navel), the **heart chakra** (in the center of the chest), the **throat chakra** (in the throat), and the **third-eye chakra** (in the center of the forehead), up to the **crown chakra** (at the top of the head). Take as much time as you need to complete your exploration of the chakras.

6. When you have "sensed" all of the energy centers, bring your focus back to your breathing. Place your hands on the receiver's feet and gently rub them to bring their consciousness back into their body. Ask the receiver to open their eyes slowly.

Remember to record any experiences in your angel notebook. This exercise may also be performed on yourself and your own chakras. If you do not feel them the first time, do not worry: the more you practice, the easier it will become to tune into the subtle bodies.

Exploring the Chakras With the Assistance of the Angelic Realms

You will have noticed when reading the section on chakras that angels and archangels have an affinity with particular chakras. We are now going to enlist the help of these heavenly beings to explore, balance, and heal the chakras.

Preparation

Make your usual preparations. If you have a particular chakra that you feel is out of balance, then choose one of the angelic oils associated with that chakra to use in your oil-burner. For instance, if you feel insecure, have feelings of "spaciness," and are unable to ground yourself, you may decide from looking at the chakra information to use benzoin or vetivert. Let your nose be your guide – only use an essential oil if you are attracted to the aroma. We instinctively know what we need. You may also put one neat drop of your chosen angelic oil into the center of the palm of one hand and then rub your hands together to distribute the oil evenly.

1. Make yourself comfortable. You may adopt a sitting position, either on some pillows on the floor or on a stool. If you wish, you may lie on the floor on a well-padded surface.

2. Focus on your body and try to visualize roots extending deep down into the earth so that you are firmly anchored.

3. Focus on your breathing and inhale and exhale slowly and deeply. As you breathe in, inhale the healing light of the angels, then, as you exhale, feel all of your tensions releasing, through your "roots," into the earth.

4. When you feel relaxed, become aware of your base chakra and visualize it glowing with a ruby-red light. Place your hands gently on your body to establish the position of this chakra. Invite Archangel Sandalphon or the angels of the earth to cleanse and heal your base chakra. Sense the heavenly presence and call upon your angel to help you feel safe, secure, and grounded in the physical world. Thank the angel for its blessing.

5. Change your focus to your sacral chakra in your lower abdomen, just below your navel. Gently rest the palms of your hands on this center. Become aware of an orange light glowing in your abdomen. Call forth Archangel Chamuel, who helps to heal rifts in relationships. Ask that you will not be clinging and possessive in your relationships, but that you will instead allow others to be who they are and to express themselves freely. If you wish to conceive, or are having problems with conception, then you may summon the angels of birth and ask to be blessed with a child. If you have been raped or sexually abused, then it is very likely that this center will be closed or "murky" in appearance. Call forth Archangel Gabriel to awaken the purification process. Ask for the sacral center to be cleansed and healed so that you will be able to open up to your sexuality once again. When you are ready, give thanks to the angels.

6. Bring your consciousness into your solar-plexus chakra, gently placing your hands on this center. Visualize it radiating energy like the warm, golden sun. If you feel full of tension, then ask Archangel Uriel and the angels of peace to descend to release you from your inner turmoils and fears and to fill your solar plexus with peace and tranquility. If you need protection from physical, sexual, or psychic attack, then ask for the protection of Archangel Michael. This mighty archangel can also restore your confidence and self-esteem and give you the courage and strength to face obstacles and make changes. When you are ready, thank your angels.

Sacral Chakra

Heart Chakra

7. Journey up into the center of your chest. Allow your hands to rest on the heart chakra and visualize a beautiful pink flower, with twelve petals unfolding in your heart center. Call forth Archangel Chamuel and ask that your heart be filled with the joy of pure, unconditional love. Ask for any negative emotions, such as jealousy, depression, guilt, bitterness, and despair, to be cleansed. Allow Raphael, who exudes the color of healing, into your heart to heal your deepest wounds. Thank your angels.

8. Focus on your throat chakra, the center of communication. Place your fingertips gently around your throat and see a blue light shining within. Visualize the throat center opening up so that you may speak your truth and be true to who you really are. Call forth Michael, the archangel of truth, who instills in you the strength and courage to face and express your truth. He enables you to cut through any pretence and to say and do what you truly want. Thank Archangel Michael for his help.

9. Bring your consciousness into the center of your forehead – the indigo, third-eye chakra. Feel this area open up as you awaken your intuition. Ask Gabriel, the archangel of guidance, to give you a vision of your true calling, your reason for being. Call Jophiel, the archangel of illumination, to enlighten you. Jophiel will bring you insight and clarity of mind.

Third Eye Chakra

10. Finally, place your hands lightly on the top of your crown chakra – your link with your higher self. Feel the violet light of this center radiating outward from the top of your head. Merge your consciousness with the high-frequency, violet light of Archangel Zadkiel and Saint Germain and request an acceleration of your spiritual development. Thank your heavenly helpers.

11. Breathe in all of the love and light of the angels and archangels. Feel the heavenly light coursing freely through your entire being. Be at one with the divine.

12. When you are ready, gradually bring your attention back to your body and focus on your breathing and your contact with the earth. Gradually become aware of your surroundings and slowly open your eyes.

See how different you feel! Write down any angelic messages or experiences that you received.

This exercise may also be carried out on a friend or partner. Try to balance your chakras on a weekly basis.

Angels
and
Crystals

Crystals have been revered since the dawn of civilization as having sacred and healing powers. The ancients were experts in their use. In the Bible, numerous crystals and gems are mentioned, including emerald, amethyst, jasper, topaz, sapphire, agate, and diamond.

Crystals have a strong affinity with the angelic realms, and a few beautiful crystals arranged on your altar will attract angelic presences. The crystals' vibrations enable us to attune to, and communicate with, our angels and archangels to receive wisdom, guidance, and healing. Although the heavenly beings are attracted to all crystals, I believe that they each have their favorites. For instance, rose quartz is like a magnet to Archangel Chamuel, who is drawn by the unconditional love that it radiates. Green crystals, such as aventurine, emerald, and jade, call forth Archangel Raphael, since he exudes the healing color of green.

As well as placing crystals in your sacred space and throughout your home to attract angels, you can also activate your own personal angel crystal as explained in this chapter. This will enable you to focus and aid your connection with the angels. Both angels and crystals are here to serve us and expand our consciousness.

Choosing a Crystal

When selecting a crystal, trust your intuition and your initial impressions. Usually, the first crystal that you are drawn to is the one for you. If you are attuned to a crystal, you may experience one or more of the following sensations.

1. Heat emanating from the crystal.
2. Cold energy.
3. Pulsing or vibrating.
4. A sensation of balance and wholeness.
5. Tingling in your hands.
6. A flow of energy that may even feel like an electric charge.

Here are two simple methods that you may find useful.

A. Intuition

1. Take a few deep breaths to relax you and clear you of all negative thoughts and emotions.
2. Focus on the crystals before you and notice if any one crystal draws your attention.
3. Pick up the crystals one by one to feel the vibrations. If you are right-handed, try using your more receptive left hand. If you are left-handed, your right hand is usually the more receptive one. If a crystal resonates with you and intuitively "feels" right, this is the one to choose.

B. Scanning

1. Shake out your hands to release any blocked energy and rub the palms of your hands together to sensitize them.
2. Breathe deeply to release any negativity and to focus your mind.
3. If you are right-handed, pass your left hand very slowly over the crystals before you. (If you are left-handed, use your right hand.)
4. You will find that you will be drawn toward the crystal that has a natural affinity with you – it will feel hot or cold, tingling, and so on.

There are many other methods that can be used, including the use of a pendulum and kinesiology (muscle-testing).

Cleansing a Crystal

It is essential to cleanse a crystal prior to use to remove any negative vibrations that it may have absorbed from anyone who has previously handled it. Here are a few simple methods.

1. Water method (this technique is usually suited to those born under a water sign). If possible, find a spring, stream, or waterfall and hold your crystal under running water. If you do not live near such a water source, use bottled spring water. If you wish, you may take your crystals down to the sea to cleanse them in salt water. However, since salt can damage the crystalline structure, thoroughly rinse your crystals in pure water afterward to remove any salt residue.

2. Earth method (particularly effective for those born under an earth sign). Bury your crystal in the ground and leave it for at least twenty-four hours. If you do not have a yard, simply fill a plant pot with earth. After you have removed your crystal, wash it thoroughly in pure spring water.

3. Fire method (highly suitable for those born under a fire sign). Surround your crystal(s) with night-lights and leave the lights for a few hours until they have completely burned out. Alternatively, light a candle and pass your crystal(s) quickly through a flame.

4. Smudge method (especially attractive for those born under an air sign). Light a smudge stick and then blow out the flame. While it is smoldering, hold your crystal(s) in the smoke, allowing the element of air to transmute any negative vibrations.

5. Flower method (suitable for all). This is my favorite method. Simply gather a few flowers or petals and place them in a clear-glass container. Bury your crystal(s) under the petals, so that they are completely covered, and leave them for approximately twenty-four hours. Try to choose flowers that match the color of your crystals – if you were cleansing rose quartz, for example, pink rose petals would be particularly effective, while lavender would be very appropriate for a purple amethyst, and so on.

Activating/dedicating Your Crystals to the Angels

Once the crystals have been cleansed, they may be dedicated to the angelic realms. You may wish to carry out a simple ceremony. Simply place the crystal(s) on your sacred altar. Light a candle and burn some essential oils. When you are relaxed, invite your angels into your sacred space. Place your hands lightly on your crystals and say a few words of dedication, such as "I dedicate these crystals to the angelic realms as a bridge between heaven and earth to deepen my connection and heighten my receptivity to the guidance of the angelic streams of consciousness."

As I have previously stated, **all** crystals can help us to gain access to the angelic domain. However, angels and archangels do have an affinity for particular crystals.

There follows an outline of the crystals that I feel are most closely connected to the archangels. However, I urge you to trust your intuition – if a crystal "feels" right, then use it!

Crystals for Connecting With Archangel Michael

Color: blue/gold

Keywords: protection, courage, strength, truth

If you wish to connect with Archangel Michael and his angels of protection, angels of courage, and angels of truth, a few suggestions are as follows.

Tiger's eye
Color: dark yellow with brown bands
Functions:
- protection from negative influences
- raises self-esteem
- helps to combat addictions

Aquamarine
Color: bluish-green
Functions:
- enables you to speak your truth
- releases stress and gives courage to face up to situations
- instills bravery

Turquoise
Color: greenish-blue
Functions:
- protection
- encourages purposeful communication
- bestows truth and dignity

Lapis lazuli
Color: brilliant blue
Functions:
- teaches you to voice your opinions
- embodies the spirit of truth
- purifies the throat chakra

Crystals for Connecting With Archangel Raphael

Color: green/deep pink

Keywords: healing, wholeness, unity

To connect with Archangel Raphael, the angels of healing, and the angels of love, I suggest the following.

Aventurine
Color: green
Functions:
*   healing and comforting
*   teaches you to show love and compassion
*   opens up the heart center

Emerald
Color: light to dark green
Functions:
*   heals all problems, especially those of the heart, chest, and the emotions
*   promotes harmony and wholeness

Chrysoprase
Color: green
Functions:
*   opens, activates, and energizes the heart chakra
*   helps to heal a broken heart
*   encourages love of oneself and others

Crystals for Connecting With Archangel Chamuel

Color: pink/orange

Keywords: unconditional love, relationships

To connect with Archangel Chamuel and the angels of love, I suggest the following.

Rose quartz
Color: pink
Functions:
- encourages unconditional love, compassion, tolerance, and forgiveness
- treats heart problems
- balances the emotional body

Kunzite
Color: pale pink
Functions:
- comforts and heals the heart (physically and emotionally)
- awakens compassion
- immune-system-booster

Crystals for Connecting With Archangel Gabriel

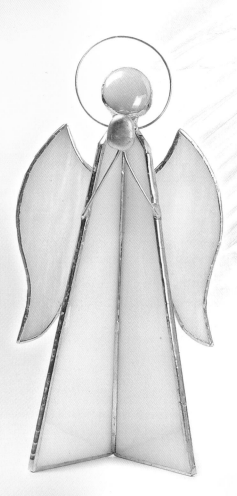

Color: indigo/white

Keywords: guidance, vision, prophecy, inspiration, purity

To connect with Archangel Gabriel and the angels of vision and prophecy, I suggest the following.

Tanzanite
Color: blue-lavender
Functions:
- facilitates visions
- allows for communication with angels, guides, ascended masters, and beings from other dimensions
- activates psychic abilities

Iolite
Color: indigo
Functions:
- a vision and prophecy stone
- opens the "third eye"
- guides you along the spiritual pathway
- awakens psychic powers
- encourages intuition

Lapis lazuli
Color: brilliant blue
Functions:
- assists in connection with your dreams
- helps attunement to the intuitive and psychic aspects
- promotes clarity of vision
- encourages purification

Blue calcite
Color: blue
Functions:
- helps you to recall channeled experiences
- clears the chakras

Crystals for Connecting With Archangel Jophiel

Color: yellow

Keywords: joy, illumination, wisdom

To connect with Archangel Jophiel and the angels of joy, I recommend the following.

Golden labradorite (sunstone)
Color: yellow
Functions:
- brings joy and laughter
- brings the sweetness back into life
- facilitates connection with your inner light

Citrine
Color: yellow
Functions:
- balances the solar plexus
- encourages joy, wonder, delight, and enthusiasm
- banishes negativity

Crystals for Connecting With Archangel Uriel

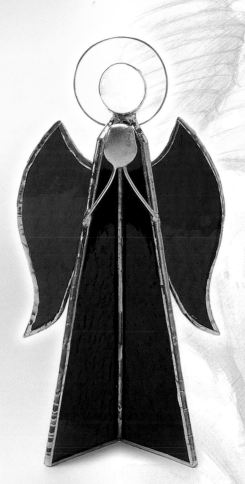

Color: gold/purple

Keywords: peace, tranquility, giving, devotion

Ametrine
(has colors of amethyst and citrine)
Color: gold/purple
Functions:

- relieves depression and negativity
- brings peace to a troubled soul
- dispels fear and phobias
- balances and soothes the emotions

Angelite
Color: lilac-blue
Functions:

- brings inner peace, tranquility, and calm
- encourages selfless devotion
- facilitates angelic attunement

Crystals for Connecting With Archangel Zadkiel

Color: violet

Keywords: transmutation of negative energy, forgiveness, tolerance

Amethyst
Color: violet/purple
Functions:

- a transformational healer
- transforms blocked energies
- encourages spiritual growth

Charoite
Color: purple
Functions:

- a spiritual transformer
- unblocks the crown chakra
- transmutes negativity

Amethyst Elestial or El

Elestials are the most extraordinary and incredibly powerful crystals. They look as if one crystal has grown over another. Elestials are known as "gifts from the angels." "El" is one of the sacred names of the living God. J. J. Hurtak says, "as we proclaim this Sacred Name, the trumpets in the angelic dimension are sounded as the doors of perception are open." This name opens the gates of vibration for different levels of divine-dialogue communication with the angelic realms.

Color: purple
Functions:

- releases karmic blockages to accelerate spiritual growth
- imparts wisdom and cosmic understanding
- Opens the "third eye" and crown chakra
- attracts Archangel Zadkiel and the Ascended Master Saint Germain with their violet flame

If you wish to invoke and work with particular angels or archangels, by simply wearing or carrying a piece of chosen crystal you will be connecting with the higher energies as you go about your everyday activities. Always try to keep a few crystals on your scared altar and to use a crystal for meditation.

Angelic "Aromacrystal" Meditation

Enter your sacred space, light a candle, and choose a crystal and an angelic oil that particularly resonate with the angel whom you wish to connect with.

Suppose, for instance, that you are experiencing throat problems. If you refer to the information on the throat chakra (page 86), you will notice that your discomfort could be connected with a failure to speak your own truth. Reflect on this. Do you perhaps always say what you think other people want to hear instead of speaking the truth? Are you true to who you really are? Notice that the Archangel Michael works with the energies of the throat chakra. Look through the list of crystals and angelic oils – which one(s) are you attracted to? Suppose your decision is:

Archangel Michael—aquamarine—blue chamomile.

You would place one drop of blue chamomile on your piece of aquamarine to create an "aromacrystal" that will align you with Archangel Michael. Now begin the meditation.

1. Sit in a comfortable position on some pillows on the floor, with your back held straight, and establish a strong connection with Mother Earth.
2. Focus on your breathing, letting go of any tension.
3. Hold your chosen "aromacrystal" between your palms, in a prayer position close to your heart chakra, for this is where the angels connect with you. Feel the powerful vibrations emanating from the crystal, coupled with the energies of the angelic oil.
4. Once you are attuned to your "aromacrystal," invite your chosen angel. Say, "I wish to connect with _____" (the likelihood is that your chosen angel may already have linked with you, having been attracted to your "aromacrystal").
5. Luxuriate in the unconditional love and light of your chosen angel. Ask for whatever guidance or healing you require.
6. Remain as long as you like in the company of your angelic beings. When you are ready to return, give thanks.
7. Become aware of your body and breathing. Slowly open your eyes..

Remember to record your experiences in your angel notebook. Cleanse the 'aromacrystal' thoroughly.

Crystals and the Chakras

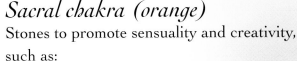

Crystals may be placed on the different chakras to balance and heal them. If the energy centers are blocked, this will result in ill health, whereas when the energy is flowing freely, we feel balanced and healthy.

For a basic chakra layout you will need seven stones – one for the color of each chakra. Select small ones, as we will be placing them on the body. Here are a few suggestions of crystals that would be particularly effective.

Base/root chakra (red)
Red stones to increase energy levels, like:

- ruby

- garnet

- red jasper

- Also: bloodstone, red calcite

Black or brown stones to provide grounding and protection, such as:

- smoky quartz

- black tourmaline

- Also: obsidian, black agate

Sacral chakra (orange)
Stones to promote sensuality and creativity, such as:

- orange calcite

- citrine

- carnelian

- topaz

- Also: amber, orange sunstone

Solar-plexus chakra (yellow)
Stones to release tension, give confidence and courage and bring joy, such as:

- citrine

- tiger's eye

- Also: ametrine, golden sunstone

Heart chakra (pink/green)

Stones to promote unconditional love and compassion, such as:

- emerald

- jade

- rose quartz

- kunzite

- Also: chrysoprase, green aventurine

Throat chakra (blue)

Stones to encourage communication and expression, such as:

- blue lace agate

- aquamarine

- turquoise

- Also: lapis lazuli, chrysocolla

Third-eye chakra (indigo)

Stones to open up the intuition, like:

- lapis lazuli

- tanzanite

- Also: iolite

Crown chakra (violet)

Stones to connect us with our higher self, such as:

- amethyst

- clear quartz

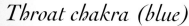

- selenite

- charoite

Chakra-balancing Treatment

Carry out the treatment with the receiver lying face up on a well-padded surface, with one pilow under their head and another under their knees. Make sure that the seven small stones that you have chosen – one for each chakra – are close to hand.

1. Ensure that you are both relaxed and grounded. Position yourself at the receiver's feet, center yourself, and take a few deep breaths to release any negativity. Gently hold the receiver's feet and imagine that roots are growing out of the soles of their feet and their spine into the earth.

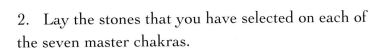

2. Lay the stones that you have selected on each of the seven master chakras.

3. Leave them there for ten to fifteen minutes to allow integration of the crystal vibration.

4. Remove the crystals. Return to the receiver's feet and gently rub their feet and lower legs to ground and balance them. Thank your angels for their assistance.

5 Cleanse your crystals.

6. When the receiver is ready, ask them to open their eyes gently.

You may, of course, carry out the suggested chakra-balancing treatment on yourself.

Angels in Your Everyday Life

Once you start connecting with your angels, you will "see" and "feel" them absolutely everywhere. You will realize that they are always with you. Angels do not only connect with us when we enter our sacred space – they are with us every moment of the day, guiding and protecting us as we perform our everyday tasks. Do not wait for an emergency or a crisis situation to invoke your angels. No job is too big or too small for the angelic beings. Whether you want to find a parking space or a lost item or your washing machine needs fixing, the angels will be happy to oblige. No request is too trivial, so why make life difficult for yourself?

The Angels of Protection

The Angels of Protection can be called upon to look after loved ones.

You can protect your home, your automobile, yourself, and your loved ones by calling forth the angels of protection.

Before going to sleep at night, ask these angels to surround your home with their loving energy of protection. They will create an invincible force field that will effectively repel any burglars or other undesirable attention.

If you have parked your automobile, especially if you are in an unfamiliar or unsafe environment, call upon the angels of protection to surround and protect it. If you run out of gas, ask for angelic protection and to be rescued quickly.

Call upon these angels to protect you when traveling.

If you find yourself in a situation in which you feel uncomfortable, invoke your angels to guard you against negative energies. As your children go off to school, visualize the angels of protection guarding them and helping them. Send angels to make your friends and family feel safe and protected.

If you are traveling, call upon the angels to protect your automobile and its occupants. When you are flying, surround the airplane with hosts of angels.

The Angel Repair Team

As I was nearing completion of this book, and on a rare occasion when the data had not recently been backed up, the hard drive of my computer suddenly crashed. It seemed inevitable that much of my work had been lost and would have to be retyped. I sent out an S.O.S. to the angels of repair and, hey presto, a few minutes later my computer was working again!

Always ask for angelic intervention for faulty mechanical and electronic devices.

Angels can help with computer, electronic and mechanical problems.

The Finding Angels

How many times have you lost your keys and felt stressed as a result? Trying to locate lost items can be a most frustrating and time-wasting experience. It therefore makes a lot of sense to ask for help from your angels.

I have heard many stories of people who have searched for hours, or even days, for missing objects, such as misplaced documents and jewelry. Eventually they have asked their angels for help and have found the item just minutes later.

Simply ask your angels, "Please help me find _____." You may hear a voice in your head telling you where to look, may have a vision of the missing object's location, or may be strongly drawn toward a particular room in which you will find the lost item. If you do not receive an instant reply, ask your angels where it is just before going to sleep. When you wake up in the morning, you may have a flash of inspiration or may find the missing article on your bedside table.

Asking for help from the Finding Angels can help locate commonly lost items.

If you lose a possession – for instance, a purse or billfold – and fear that it is not in the house, summon Archangel Michael to watch over it. Next, ask the finding angels to help you to remember where you lost it. Once you have located your belongings, you should find everything intact!

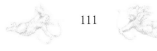

The Parking Angels

Whenever you need a parking space, try invoking an angel of parking. As you set out on your journey, tell your angel approximately where you would like your parking space to be and your angel will try to clear the space for you. The results are amazing – you will easily find a space with the assistance of the parking angels.

The Shopping Angels

Calling upon the Shopping Angels can help you save money on your purchases!

Next time you go shopping, ask your angels to accompany you and you will notice a remarkable difference: they can save you a lot of time, energy, and money. I remember at Christmas, my daughter, Chloe, saw a quill pen in the window of a jeweler and decided that it would be the perfect gift for her history teacher, who runs a calligraphy club at her school. We went in to buy it and she was bitterly disappointed when the manager told us that he had purchased it at Edinburgh Castle, hundreds of miles away in Scotland, and that it was for display purposes only. Chloe was so disheartened that I called on the angels. Thankfully, they immediately came to the rescue. The name of a store popped into my head and on our arrival there we were amazed and delighted to find exactly what we wanted: a quill pen with a red feather on the end. Our angels made it so easy for us and saved us lots of time and energy.

As for saving us money, just last week I was shopping for some pants for my daughter. As I arrived at the checkout to pay for them, the assistant closed the cash register (it was closing time), so I asked her to put the pants aside for me. A few days later, I was on my way to collect them and a little "voice" in my head urged me to look in another store. To my amazement, there was the same pair of pants at a greatly reduced price. So next time you shop, let the angels find the bargains!

In the supermarket, if there is an item on your shopping list that you cannot find, ask your angel and you will soon find yourself in the right aisle. If you know that you have forgotten something, but can't remember what, ask an angel and you will quickly remember what it is. Incidentally, always try to bless and give thanks for your food. The light of the angelic blessings will purify and energize it, making it much more healthy and nutritious.

The Angels of Direction

Angels can help you find your way.

I have never had a very good sense of direction and am by no means the best map-reader in the world! Whenever I go anywhere, even if I am traveling to another country, it never occurs to me to take a map. I simply ask the angels to direct me to my destination. This method, to everyone's surprise and amusement, has never yet failed me. Sometimes I am divinely guided down all sorts of back streets that only a local could possibly know. At other times I am directed to pull over to the side of the road. Regardless of the time of day or night, "someone" will immediately appear and tell me exactly where to go. Strangely enough, when I look around, I often find that they have disappeared into thin air.

I have previously stated that angels have never incarnated and cannot become humans and that humans can never evolve into angels. However, I feel certain that angels can adopt a "temporary" human form if necessary. I have experienced this happening many times and I know of many others who have had similar experiences.

I hope that you have enjoyed working with your angels and urge you to remember to call on them and include them in all aspects of your daily life. Remember that the angels patiently await your call. It is up to you to request their assistance.

Ask and it will be given you. Seek and you will find. Knock and it will be opened unto you.

Matthew 7:7.

The Wheel of Angels

The wheel of angels is a tool for assisting you to connect and work with your angels. It is an intuitive way of discovering the inspiration and guidance that the angelic realms are trying to communicate to you right now. It will enable you to focus upon particular aspects of your life and encourage you gently along the spiritual pathway. It is also lots of fun to work with!

Using the Wheel of Angels

1. Sit in a comfortable position with the wheel of angels in front of you or on your lap. Close your eyes and become aware of your breathing. Take a few deep breaths, inhaling all of the love and light of the angelic beings and exhaling all of your stress and tension.

2. Place the palm of your hand down flat on the wheel of angels and circle your hand over the page nine times, moving in a clockwise direction. This will infuse your energy into the wheel.

3. Leaving your hand on the page, connect with your favorite angel(s) and mentally or verbally request their assistance in making your selection.

4. Keeping your eyes closed, lift your hand a few inches and allow it to hover over the page, still keeping your palm facing downward. Now either ask your angel(s) to give you general guidance or ask a specific question about a particular aspect of your life. For instance, a general question could be, "Please show me what I should focus on next." The question you ask is entirely up to you.

5. Allow your middle finger to drop downward, so that it is pointing toward the wheel, and gently lower it on to the page.

6. Open your eyes to discover your angelic message. All of the information that you will need to interpret your selection is contained within the next few pages.

7. After you have finished consulting your wheel of angels, place your hand, palm facing downward, on the wheel and thank your angel(s) for their guidance and blessings. If a friend or partner wants to use the wheel, ask your angel(s) to clear away your energy from the wheel so that it does not interfere with their selection.

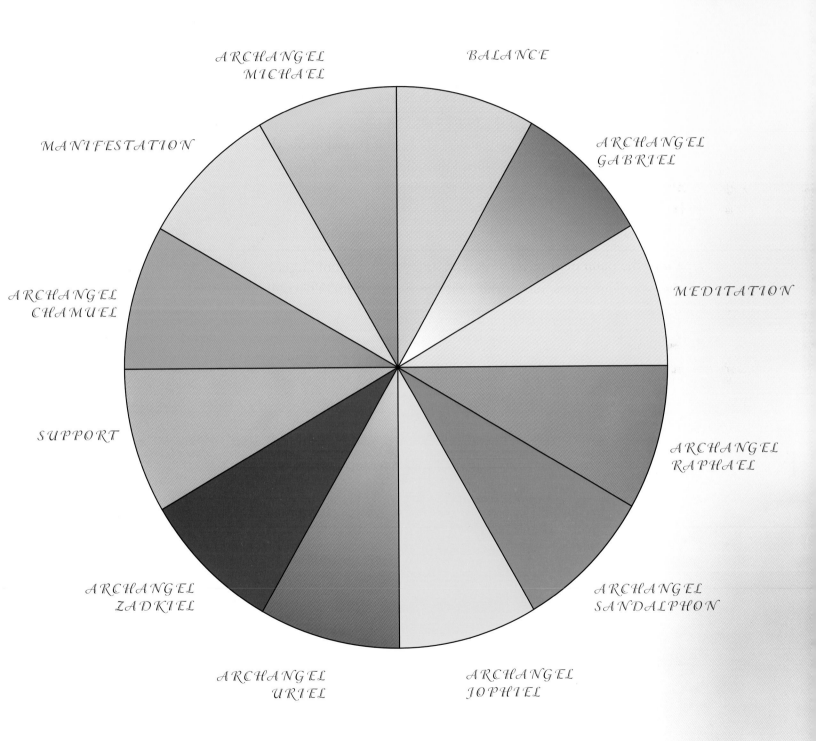

BALANCE

ARCHANGEL
MICHAEL

ARCHANGEL
GABRIEL

MANIFESTATION

MEDITATION

ARCHANGEL
CHAMUEL

ARCHANGEL
RAPHAEL

SUPPORT

ARCHANGEL
ZADKIEL

ARCHANGEL
SANDALPHON

ARCHANGEL
URIEL

ARCHANGEL
JOPHIEL

Interpreting the Wheel of Angels

Archangel Michael

Meaning:

- protection
- courage
- truth

Archangel Michael is letting you know that he is here to protect you physically, emotionally, and spiritually. He wants you to know that you are safe and secure in his powerful presence. Fear not, for he is with you. Choosing Michael can indicate that there are some changes (job, relationship, and so on) that you need to make in your life. Whatever obstacles stand in your way, Michael will fill you with the courage and strength to make these changes.

Archangel Michael is the symbol of truth and urges you to look deep inside yourself to discover your true nature and be true youself.

Archangel Raphael

Meaning:

- healing
- wholeness

If Archangel Raphael has drawn you close to his side, this indicates that you have natural healing abilities. If there is someone around you who needs healing of the body, mind, or spirit, Raphael will assist you in helping them. He asks you to surround them with beautiful, healing light and then observe the benefits.

Choosing Raphael may also indicate that a relationship, a difficult situation, or a health problem concerning you will soon be healed. Do not fear, for you will feel balanced and whole again.

Archangel Chamuel

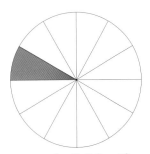

Meaning:

- love
- nurturing
- relationships

Archangel Chamuel embodies the principle of unconditional love. He urges you to love yourself, "warts and all," for if you are unable to love yourself you will not be able to love others. Chamuel asks you to look deep into your heart and release any negative emotions that you may be holding on to. Let go of these old wounds and your heart will overflow with the love of the divine.

Archangel Chamuel will assist you in moving on from past relationships and will help to heal any rifts in your current relationships. He reminds you not to be possessive and clinging. If you love someone, you should give them the freedom to be who they are. Try not to stifle, suffocate, or control them.

Archangel Chamuel wants you to know that he is always present and ready to hold you in a loving embrace.

Archangel Gabriel

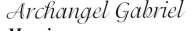

Meaning:

- guidance
- prophecy
- purity

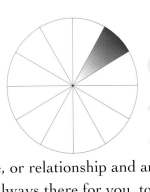

Perhaps you have chosen Archangel Gabriel because you are thinking of changing your job, home, or relationship and are unsure of the consequences. Gabriel is indicating that he is always there for you, to guide you through the changes that lie before you. Maybe you feel unfulfilled and dissatisfied with your life. If so, Archangel Gabriel is here to help you to discover your soul pathway. Ask for his guidance to find your true reason for being.

If you are drawn to Gabriel, it is likely that you have the gift of prophecy and clairvoyance. Consciously try to open up your third-eye chakra – you will be amazed at what you see!

Finally, Archangel Gabriel embodies the quality of purity. Maybe you need to pay attention to your physical body by avoiding toxins and taking exercise? Gabriel will help you to rid yourself of the impurities and to steer clear of junk food. He will also help you to clear your mind of impure, negative thoughts and will assist you in purifying your emotions.

Archangel Jophiel

Meaning:

- illumination
- joy

Archangel Jophiel urges you to pay attention to any new thoughts that come into your mind in the near future. You may be uncertain about a situation or a person in your life. Jophiel is indicating to you that you will be experiencing flashes of inspiration. All will be revealed to you.

Jophiel also wishes to bestow on you great light and joy. He wants to bring fun and laughter into your life. Do not spend all of your time working – relax more and enjoy the wonders of existence.

Whenever you feel down and fed up, Jophiel reminds you that he is here to light up your life.

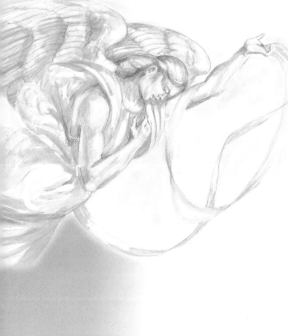

Archangel Uriel

Meaning:

- peace
- service

Archangel Uriel brings to you the quality of peace. He is here to help you to deal with your inner conflicts. Do you feel irritated and angry? Do you find it difficult to switch off your thoughts? Are you having trouble sleeping? Do you have a volatile relationship with someone? Archangel Uriel is here to remind you that whenever you feel stressed and agitated he is here to purify your solar plexus of discord and fill you with peace and tranquility.

Archangel Uriel also embodies the quality of service. Uriel wishes you to open up your eyes to the joy of service to others rather than working for purely personal gain. We all have gifts to contribute to humanity. Call on Uriel so that you may realize the work that you were born to do.

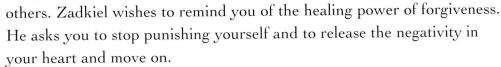

Archangel Zadkiel

Meaning:

- forgiveness
- transmutation of negative energy

If you have chosen Archangel Zadkiel, it may be that you are being too hard on yourself or on others. Zadkiel wishes to remind you of the healing power of forgiveness. He asks you to stop punishing yourself and to release the negativity in your heart and move on.

Archangel Zadkiel is the archangel of transformation and transmutation. By choosing him you are expressing a desire to accelerate your spiritual development. Call forth Zadkiel to help you to strengthen your link with the divine. He can also help you to transmute negative energy into positive energy and to heal traumas from past lives.

If you choose Archangel Zadkiel, you wish to strengthen your spiritual link with the divine.

Archangel Sandalphon

Meaning:

- grounding
- security

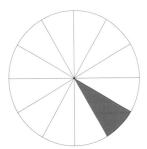

Archangel Sandalphon is very much connected with the earth energies, and you have chosen him to remind you of the importance of being grounded and of being in **this** world. He will help you to establish a secure link between heaven and earth. Archangel Sandalphon is very much aware that it is sometimes difficult to be in the physical world, yet it is an experience that we have chosen and we are very privileged and blessed to be here at this important time. Archangel Sandalphon also offers you security. Those who feel insecure will often seek security outside themselves. They think that if they achieve yet another goal this will make them feel secure. Sandalphon teaches us to look within ourselves and reminds us that we are safe and secure in the presence of our angels.

Balance

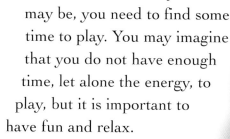

If you have chosen this aspect, the angels of balance want you to know that life should not be all work and no play. You need to establish a balance in your life. However busy your schedule may be, you need to find some time to play. You may imagine that you do not have enough time, let alone the energy, to play, but it is important to have fun and relax.

Make sure that you have time to relax and take time for yourself.

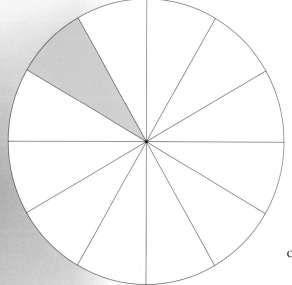

Manifestation

If this is your choice, then prepare for the transformation that will soon arrive. You have been thinking about making changes in your life and now is the time to put your ideas into action. The angels will help you to transform your thoughts into tangible form. You should pay careful attention to the signs, and also to your thoughts. Doors will be opening before you and new opportunities will come your way. Trust the signs that are given to you by the angels and your dreams will come true.

Support

Your angels want you to know that you are surrounded by divine love and blessings. It is easy to forget this if you are in a difficult situation and cannot see a way forward. Regardless of the challenges that you are facing, the angels are reminding you to call upon them to help to resolve your problems. They wish to remind you to talk to them frequently. The angels are full of love and are here to guide you when you feel lost, comfort you when you feel sad and alone, and protect you at all times. They are **always** by your side.

Be assured that the angels are surrounding you with their divine love at this very moment!

Spend time in meditation. The more you meditate, the easier it will be for you to commune with your angels.

Meditation

The angels are showing you that you need to spend some time on your own in quiet meditation. Practice meditation as often as you can, and in the stillness you will receive angelic messages and inspiration. The more you quieten your mind, the easier it will be for you to hear your angels.

As you meditate, the angels wish you to reflect on your life and to listen to your heart and follow your intuition. There is an aspect of your life that you need to let go of or change. The angels of meditation are urging you to reach out to them so that they may reveal your deepest dreams and desires.

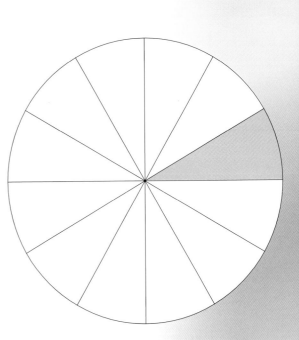

Useful Addresses

The angel website of Denise Whichello Brown:
www.angel-therapy.com

For details of Denise's archangel blends, angelic oils, crystals and 'aromacrystals', wheel-of-angels chart, angel workshops, and more, visit:
www.denisebrown.co.uk

For information on workshops and training in complementary medicine under the personal supervision of Denise Whichello Brown:
Beaumont College of Natural Medicine
MWB Business Exchange
23 Hinton Road, Bournemouth, Dorset, BH1 2EF, United Kingdom.

Credits and Acknowledgements

I would like to thank my loving husband once again, both for typing this manuscript for me and for all of his patience.

I also thank my beloved children, Chloe and Thomas, for being so understanding when I was writing this book.

I give thanks for the profound wisdom of Alice Bailey, J. J. Hurtak, and Joshua Stone. Finally, I thank the angelic realms and Sai Baba for their guidance.

Picture Credits

Angel illustrations by Peter Mallison
Photographs pp 16, 17, 110, 111 © Stockbyte 2001
Angel wheel © Denise Whichello Brown